GW01319553

ASSARACUS

A Journal of Gay Poetry
Issue 4

SiblingRivalryPress

Alexander, Arkansas
www.siblingrivalrypress.com

Assaracus
A Journal of Gay Poetry
Issue 4: October 2011
ISBN: 978-1-937420-02-4
ISSN: 2159-0478
Bryan Borland, Editor
Copyright © 2011 by Sibling Rivalry Press, LLC

Cover Art: Orange and Red Portrait by James Kaminski. Used by Permission.

A special thanks to Philip F. Clark, Jim Kangas, and Carl Miller Daniels for their help with this issue.

Sibling Rivalry Press, LLC
13913 Magnolia Glen Drive
Alexander, AR 72002

www.siblingrivalrypress.com

ASSARACUS

HOLLAND
WALTER

an island known for boys

Walter Holland, Ph.D., is the author of three books of poetry: *Circuit* (Chelsea Station Editions, 2010), *Transatlantic*, (Painted Leaf Press, 2001), *A Journal of the Plague Years: Poems 1979-1992* (Magic City Press, 1992) as well as a novel, *The March* (Masquerade Books, 1996; re-published by Chelsea Station Editions, 2010). His short stories have been published in *Art and Understanding, Harrington Gay Men's Fiction Quarterly, Rebel Yell,* and *Mama's Boy: Gay Men Writing About Their Mothers.* Some of his poetry credits include: *Antioch Review, Art and Understanding, Barrow Street, Bay Windows, Body Positive, Christopher Street, Chiron Review, The Cream City Review, Found Object, Men's Style, Pegasus, Phoebe,* and *Poets for Life: 76 Poets Respond to AIDS.* He lives in New York City and works as a physical therapist.

SKINNY DIPPING

Jeans by a creek and the glassy surface of the water
You didn't blush

Dumping your clothing beside, climbing on a rock
To recline,

As the sun took you into its hot glare. I was aware
Of my eyes

Turning away and the trembling of my hands on
The buttons of my shirt,

The cool of the air on my skin. How do I begin
To tell you

That I loved you, whatever love could mean
Between boys.

The soft mud squishing on my feet underneath
As I followed you blindly

From shade into light,
Afraid, afraid of what I couldn't explain.

WORKMEN

Do they envy the idleness of our morning walk?
The way we move carelessly along, our small talk
and the cash we have taken from the ATM.
Do they feel odd, on this island predominantly full of men?
are they self-conscious of how they look or what they wear?
How they shave their beards or comb their hair?
No, it's all in a day's work, I'd imagine, for most of them,
and given their manly swagger they blend
right in — trying to play their part —
unaware that some of them will break the heart
of many a man. There's money here
whether it's straight or queer
doesn't seem to matter. It's love'em or leave'em alone —
a policy that's built or torn down many an island home.

FOR MARIE

Landlady of an island known for boys
you wore bright nightgowns, gazing off the deck
and hollered down to lovers when annoyed
or spoke to goldfish with tones of sad regret.
First party girl of summers from the past
and chronicler of drunken times and drugs
a sixties swinger's marriage then the fast
and fatal end of the husband, with a shrug
you'd toss a giant joint to boys below
who cried out every night for your supply
and brought you cash for what you might bestow
and suffer bawdy tales of those who'd died.
Now sickness takes you from the glamorous house
and, without answer, boys still seek you out.

FIRE ISLAND, MAY 98

These graftings of new urban dreams
a cube of lawn in marshy woods
the house of glass lit up with lights
that advertises and confines

this world's addiction for design
transparency and all the rest.
The clutter of an urban mind
projected on a pile of sand

a casual carefreeness in cash
confirmed by scattered morning trash
an urban sprawl of luxury's litter
of dinners planned and parties played

the bitter-sweet that follows us
and brightens out our days
with morning's rituals that absolve
sophisticated summer sins —

we mark our time-shares on the beach
draw kilowatts of hazy sun
and leisure late until we long
for what the papers print and praise

consumer culture — opera — plays,
with tired ambitions that affirm
the little vanities we've earned
from beauty rented, beauty owned.

CLUB CULTURE

Even then as now, you descend
into the gossip of old times,
the diminutive effect of look and
languor. Once you knew the guide book
of those shadowy palaces, your
star-crossed path through poppy fields
the fabled road over a psychedelic rainbow
and its smoke and mirror illusion.
Name the conditions and principles
of the night, who were cordoned off
and who were ushered in: name, money
and miracles, the price for your
admission. It was an addiction
to the scene and its delirious celebrity,
fifteen-minutes of fame and the fairy
tale begun when the clock struck glamour.
All one needed was to reek of obscurity
and to find in the twisted tinsel
of that age, some dark, velveteen
corner of the mind, plush, dramatic,
degenerate. Enough to let us in
to the intersanctum which proved
to be elusive as light
shadows bounded by
nothing but the dark gilded longing to be
more.

Walter Holland

MORNING OF THE MARCH
(The Gay and Lesbian March on Washington, October, 1987)

Sunrise over Washington, the roof tops and
ledges soft and gray under renewed light —
blue, open and wide the sky. Half-asleep I listened to church

bells peal, salutations to the dawn, and what
began as clouds parting, admitting the fuller
light, some ponderous slow and majestic

movement, the steady decorum of thought.
One morning you feel how great a shared faith is
its mighty hold on dignity, how some are chosen

to fight alone the battle of inequality. Those
of that room half numbered now, of grave and
cloth and minutes fled. A photograph of who we

were, friends and lovers of the march, encircled arms,
excited grins, some folded bedding on a floor,
our protest in that civil war of forced allegiance,

legal shame, indentured to a social system
repressive of our years. To touch beneath October
trees, like men who love, beyond disease, beyond

the wide and vacant street, the angered shouts and
rising storm of activists and stricken men, their mottled
skin and thinning arms, gaunt soldiers of the crisis come;

and now a veteran to those times, what of my stories
gone and lived, we spread our flags of grief and name
across great fields before a dome, and staked our claim for love

unbound, some fabrics shorn of lone dissent, near holy scorn
and righteous lies, when we were young above the grass
our crossings through the quilted paths of lovers lost

and lovers near, some lonely anthem in my mind, a parted
country whole again, a union like the one I've found
and we the sentries of that hope, the young men of that morning.

THE BEAUTY OF MEN

Half a look at him in the street confirmed
that we grow old hungering for young bodies.
Clear-eyed and taut of frame, legs sleek by
running and with broad hulking arms, he knew
and I knew that I would consume him if I could,
limb lapped by tongue over the smooth pelt of his skin.
I wanted to feel his boyish power, be pinned under him —
chest, breath and what I knew of his sturdy, stocky
frame. I wanted to be pierced by him and see
his panting, half-boy blush over the snow-white
of back and thighs, the perfect indentation of
bone, shallow, young, smooth, arched, plunged
by the long action of his sweating form; but he crossed
the road to the other side and the moment slipped by.

TATTOO

Bent over near the shower, he was all back
warm and curving, flushed from the steam
and huge, so built and broad that
his spine made a deep furrow down to his lean
perfect haunches on the bench. Slick
and wet, the striking colors of the pattern snaked
across his skin, a dragon green and red flicked
its tongue of dotted black on pink. From his sleek waist
the towel fell and spread, the dragon upward
clung to that massive hairless armor, at strong labor
it spanned his oaken neck to round shoulders hard
and ivory white. To ride that sleek torso and to savor
its serpent's column under my slippery hands —
the flames of that beast licking at the man.

THE WALK
For Howard

(Soapstone State Park,
walk with Val and Joe)

The four of us complete
this vision of gay men at middle-age.
I never truly imagined how I would end —
married with wife or alone in a room —
the incomplete fears of the boy
for how love, age and the future
would be — but here along the autumn slopes
of the trail past the wooded homes
enormous and wealthy
steeped in the look of suburban
ease (the veneer of family values), now I know,
can see, what age has brought me — sex, acceptance,
trust — the troubling questions still not answered
but tempered by so much time and life
beside a man I've chosen to love, sharing
a home up north in the City, a mere three
rooms, two cats and books that threaten
to overtake us — the gray
hairs of his head marking this history,
receding hairlines — could it be we have
lived out these years, traveled and talked
argued and kissed, to appear this couple
at late afternoon wandering the fringe
of the forest past the glowing lawns of homes
whose nostalgic recreations of nurture
share sentimental affinities with
an American dream of storybook times — man —
woman — marriage? Foreign now this system of
thinking, long out of that myth, we've lived apart
in our own definition of belonging. Not a fifties' America
we saw at birth, or the sixties rebellion we
lived on our own, but now wedded to him,
how strange to confront a fate that's been ours
alone; how beautiful, too, and blessed
that thinking I'd have no home at all,
we've made our place like all the rest.

THE DRAG PERFORMANCE

This city block at summer, past Redden's funeral home,
the place I last saw your body. Fourteenth now in summer's heat,
I'm heading west toward the old Anvil, the place you roamed
about in the seventies — the packing district, hunks of meat
hanging on hooks over docks of sawdust, where men at night
had sex in trucks and fronted the warehouses. A drag queen giving a show,
a cause for celebrity, a downtown following — I head to the theater, in sight
the restaurants, cafes, condos, urban renewal spreading now below
Chelsea. I remember you in gloves, running mascara in streams of black
and a packed room with the lilt of your voice as you spun some Haitian
voodoo spell. Tall priestess garbed in makeshift sparkles, dead queens back
then could not be buried anywhere else but Redden's, fear ran
so rampant during the plague that corpses lay unclaimed for days
no one dared to carry them away.

MCGAHA
TELLY

geography of love

Telly McGaha is a native Kentuckian with an unhealthy obsession of place. He idolizes Charm City, sees Chocolate City as a demagogue, has a forlorn bittersweet longing for Falls City, reveres the Crescent City, views the Queen City as his lifelong nemesis, and has a love/hate relationship with the Bluegrass State, where he, his partner, and son currently reside. The poems here make up a collective body of work called "Geography of Love."

www.tellymcgaha.com

GIGNESTHAI

Before you, there were only guesses,
wild abandonment of my senses.
In a void world without form
where our light and darkness melded;
how quickly we built a firmament.

Yours is the heat of the big bang,
easy fire burning between your loins.
Your eyes, universes afire,
a burgeoning sun – the only one
into which I gaze without going blind.

My body trembles in traversing
your galaxy black skin, the only
space through which I travel.
My dark and bright heavens,
you and these places have consumed me.

In a not too distant future,
before we collapse into the other
and cease to exist,
may we create a kind of canon
from which good things are born,

a star for others to follow.

LOVE AMONG THE PELICANS

Vacherie

You warn me:
Don't lean so far
over the well. Under
my blue eyes, you steal
a stick of cane. We laugh
among lingering ghosts:
house, cabins
histories, dissonance.

You lay siege to fields
while I seize a lazy day.
In our place together,
we are altering time.

739 Bourbon – 800 Bourbon

Do you love me when we are apart,
    as if I were culpable pleasures
enjoyed between guilt and penance?
    Am I nothing more than a John
the Conqueror hiding out in pockets,
    or a concealed lodestone used for luring
massages, Marines, and paramours?
    Come to me with dressed letters, black
cat bones, and make three crosses upon my chest:
    What your finger will feel is real,
                    without superstition.

LOVE IN THE LAND OF YELLOWJACKETS

NKU

Still barely a man
offering loaves of fishes,
okra and curry,
we eat
and I love
the sensuousness
of boiled dumplings – and lust
for the filling of your tongue.

Land Between the Lakes

Our love moves
like yonder buffalo:
slow, deliberate,
cautious, alluring,
a curiosity drawing near.
    Why not ford the river
and explore another shore,
no longer afraid to feel?

Garrard

Devoid of you, I am almost lost
to dark dreams built for dwelling.
Awake,   reach for your absence.
Watch your silhouette glow
in the monitored hue:

It is only a chasm
of hallway between us.

Garrard, revisited

You feel gone to me,
     a sort of civilization
almost achieved.
      My life spent reaching for you:
researching rumors of golden cities,
        investigating mythical fountains
so as to not miss your clues, but
      you came slow as Colombo, retreated
quick as a Caribbean sea
      from the whitest shore.

LOVE IN THE OLD LINE

Edgewater

We charted the course;
the stars shift two months
and there is no you.

I hear the South
River struggling
into the sea.
A lonesome horn
and a longing light
search for the other.

I came to you,
not for trading,
but for keeping,
yet today I peddle my misery.

Studio

You come stealthily,
brown eyes wide,
barely rustling bushes,
    deceitful before roaring:
I crack inside trying
    to disguise
        the smell of fear.
        I lay silent, feigning content
    in the fevered warmth
of misery.

Saint Paul

You think it first,
and I see it coming:
    And out of his mouth
    comes a sharp sword.
I am smitten by that name,
and vengeance is yours.

Shadyside

The cruelest trickery of the gods
in aligning two souls at a point
specific and tidy,
unkempt and unclean,
where shoes are piled upon
well-organized others
or   disheveled blankets
are tossed throughout tediously
cleaned rooms.
Our lives: meticulously unruly.
One part of the balance swings
                    wildly
beleaguered with carelessly
cast away laundry.
The other hangs still and stable,
weighed down with
precisely
folded
pants.
Two hearts,
one reserved,   one f r e e ,
mock the gods,
beating them
at their own trickery.

LOVE ON AN ISLAND

Clarenden

I am drunk on orange
Sunsets, and in a week
I will be drunk on white
rum, eager to eat the goat
I saw decapitated
and the fishes
wrapped in last week's newspaper.
On this island, I am
renewed, rejuvenated, reborn.
In your place, I remember,
without ever seeing,
how far you have come
to be in my world today.

Girls Town

I ease back to you
because I know
you will be scared
to face the darkness
and known dangers
of the bush alone,
where turning corners
become dead ends
or crossing crossroads
may turn into the Styx.

A child peddles by, calling out
his warning: *Duppy! Duppy!*

I search for you in the distance.
Your eyes alight with surprise:
    I have traveled alone,
    daring dangers you will not,
    coming only for you,

my almost Eurydice, confessing,
without saying a word,
fear and wonder, love and admiration.
We have traversed worlds to be together.

Trelawny

I flow with you,
moving upstream.
The shallowness is wide
yet rough, but I find
fragments of you,
your misplaced pieces,
and the water cleanses
and confirms what this island
                              will not.

Yardie

In the darkness of night,
    shielded by banana leaves,
your arm wraps around my waist.

The moon and midnight breezes
    cannot cool the passion,
and only the mango branches

can mask the sound of breathing.
    Beautiful island lover,
long have I been longing for you.

And your colonization has brought
    to my own exile ample kisses, lilting
words, and winter hibiscus.

Discovery Bay

Lost in the beauty
and broadness
of your nose –
wide as Africa – I wonder:

Why has a king not launched
    a thousand ships to colonize
the darkness of your eyes?

I find in the savage beating of your heart,
the deepness of your mouth,
and the warmth of your touch,
my own habitude and habitat.

LOVE AMONG LORDS AND LADIES

Prince George's

Understand me
   As a centaur:
When angry, my quarrel
   Is off aim, but strives
Always towards morning
   Kisses, protection, and caring
Through my
   Often misplaced skies.

14th Floor & then Lombard

And now I am awakened
as the sun rises and casts
golden nets over our skyscrapers
I make my way through the crowds
gliding like those bouncing buses
and determined pedestrians
unknown to anyone
except the one that matters
In a city so big
I feel larger than life

Baltimore

The month Isabelle arrived
and let our harbor eat the city,
you were new here and not adjusting.

*(How I wrapped myself around you tightly
the night she ran ashore
and how your laughter roared
louder than rattling windows.)*

I fearfully clung to you,
as if your Jamaicanness
spoke hurricane
and could protect me,

but your condescension
in saying,

"*this* is no hurricane"
only scared me more.

This thing respects no boundaries.
I have held you tightly,
you will slip free;
the decision to anchor my arm

around your waist is mine, but I hesitate,
thinking instead of life without you,
not having this option to reach
or draw myself up as if we were one.

The month Isabelle arrived
and let our harbor eat the city,
you were new here and not adjusting,
                         but we made it

strolling strongly hand-in-hand
beneath duct-taped windows
as if our lives depended upon it.

Charles Street

We glide as two spirits
down the forlorn street,
beyond the now dark cathedral,
statues of men upon horses, and
Washington high atop his mount
to where the street returns to life.

I will wait for you
when we are no longer
earthly

and still I will see
your own monumental
fierceness, joy, and tenderness
in those hardened eyes.

Nam King

I wonder what it is like without you
and wander as far as Nam Kang to see,
but only because the possibility is real.

My low-hanging heart weighs me down the stairs
and I watch as brown faces stare
but all I see is your black face

looking over hovering hands, struggling
to raise the kimchi jigue by the spoonfuls.
Your voice echoes: the flame is too hot.

I imagine the coldness outside,
barely bearable for one.

My belly rounds with OB and panchan,
but I will ascend, if only onto the street,
not like an eagle soaring over the Potomac,
but the phoenix as she crashes down,
her heart loyal to this pain.

Harford Road

We descend from evergreens,
south of north, through the green lands.

This windowless car, like a snake charmer,
lures the cool air and as the naja naja

unfurls from her basket, you sleepily
and charmingly coil yourself within

the blanket we used to stay warm
that May night in the mountains

while I warm myself in your unaware
presence. I said I loved you

and you do not hear, but instead,
hopefully, dream of me saying it
in a thousand voices.

LOVE IN THE BLUEGRASS

Saylor Woods

We kiss, Castor and Pollox,
hovering above frozen firmaments,
collecting parting embraces
as if they were medallions
safeguarding our journey
into the early morning midnight world
where hungry, unseen eyes burn
from beyond the forest line,
their own lips parting and wet
with darkened ambition.

Then comes the sun, ever crowding
darkness into western horizons,
giving safe passage, making moist
talismans unnecessary, so long
as Perseus has not yet spied Andromeda.

Spencely

She said:
This is an adult house;
you moved from Baltimore
and grew up.
Yes, we traded decked out dance floors
and strobe lights for a flagstone patio
and starry nights.
The bum-bum-bum of thumping tones
is now de-dum-de-deum of singing toads;
we are far removed
from those youthful days. A gourmet kitchen
takes the place of fine dining; no more martinis
in cosmopolitan bars.
These days we shake and make our own fun;
Our sun has slid from noon, nearing evening
but it is not yet the night and in that I find peace
and quiet mingling
with excitement. After all, there is no more
slipping and sliding on baby oiled shower curtains
spread out like a picnic
blanket, but you remind me still: We can find a thrill
with the right attire.
                    Much remains to be explored.

Insurance Appraiser in Kenton County

You call me on the phone
to get directions to my home,
but when a black man answers the door,
there is a sudden surprised tone:

"Are you Telly?" No.
"Are you a renter?"

(because the house is too much for a black man to own
or because the area is too rural for a black man to call it home?)

"You own this house,"
you repeat with doubt.

(does it seem so bizarre that a black man could come so far
from poverty, from the city, from where other black folks are?)

Now, your coup de grace:
"You own this house
with Telly?"

(do you wonder if I'm black, or just feel two men
should not be living here because it is a sin?
Or, are you embarrassed the least little bit at all?)

Just remember: It was you that was lost before your call.

TBD

Remembering Prior to Reincarnation

You, my partner
in business, life, and love
for the past decade
and perhaps the furthest
reaches of time,
recall this:
the tightness of a hand,
the taste of tears,
the warm breathing,
all this comfort that surrounds,
perfectly gift-wrapped modesty,
simple things to carry with you always

For when the day comes
that we cannot be side by side
as the minutes burn into
sterilized ethereality
of some hospital far away
lacking in happily-ever-afters.
Save these for when
morals, laws, and rules keep our final
breaths, seconds, and pains apart,
and take them with you
to that next space.

After one is burned and one is buried,
there will need to be remembering
as we search each other out
for the next lifetime.

On Crossing the Styx

In those final moments
when my breath clings to this earth,
my lashes flutter,
and my soul loosens from its chaff,
I will confide in you my secrets:

Where the pepper is hidden
and the clothes are put away;

how to properly load a dishwasher;
what oils you should eat
and which fishes you should not,
that you must not veer onto 50
too quickly, or you end up in Chillicothe;
and, in which aisle they sell your favorite plums.

I will worry for loving you too much
and my death wish will be to not have held
                         your hand as tightly.

Ragnarok

Two stars so distant
they appear to be one burning;
among others, we are
our own constellation:
    A legend to which lovers aspire,
    two distant people,
    one a warrior who slays the beast,
    a forsaken lover cast off into other galaxies,
    a sacrificial archer and musician rejoicing,
from which all other
good universes might spring.

VIANESE
ISAIAH

what can break you

Isaiah Vianese is author of the chapbook *Stopping on the Old Highway* (Recycled Karma Press, 2009), and his poems have appeared in *Ballard Street Poetry Journal, Blue Collar Review, The Fourth,* and *Moon City Review.* He writes book reviews for *Reclusive Bibliophile* and lives in New York, where he teaches writing.

ivianesefromyes.blogspot.com

PRELUDE: SUPERSTAR

Mother's music taught me romance,
sitting on the dining room floor with her cassettes.

Those Saturday mornings, Karen Carpenter
hummed through the radio the weak, low tones

of hunger, frailty, the loneliness of being left
by a man for his guitar, the road.

Karen taught me about beds filling up in every town
with breasts, hands, navels, voices of different pitch —

taught me that each syllable was unique to those women
and foreign to her, to me, in a small New York town

listening and waiting for the love to start.

IT WAS NOT SEX

It was the living room carpet,
six gin and tonics spread between us,
the skin that was yes, so soft, the hair curled
around my fingers, mint-scented lips.
It was your shirt off, mine, and touch.
It was the way you said *Oh, your body*,
the way I said *I always wanted*,
but it was not sex — not this.
It was what could be held in cave of body,
in mouth, in gentle cave of hand,
the head thrown back,
the whiskered face littered with kisses,
but it was not sex. I want to be clear.
It was not sex at all, but something
we were making, and what we continued
to make hours later, talking,
the rest of the town sleeping,
but us — your beautiful form dressed again,
your form pulled back from mine.

SEX WITHOUT LOVE

has never been my skill.
Each one — even those I was not
supposed to love — I led
by the hand to a room

you could call that sweet word.
There we built a new
machine — with its many arms,
legs, its two sets of lips

touching, touching,
and that instrument let love
out into the air as breath,
sweat, choruses spoken over

and over (*Yes* he said *Yes*)
and the night taking them
away like prayers rising up
out of our plain sight.

LAUNDRY

I fold my lover's laundry, though
he is not here and has fallen for a Russian
whose accent makes him sway

(*Baby, is there music playing
where you are?*)

but I still fold the briefs, wool socks,
hang his shirts in the closet coded by color,
just as he likes, because sometimes

(*A song about cars sings from the radio,
the room is empty, the bed made.*)

— even if a bit too late — you realize
how much you need a man, how much
you can, and how much you cannot let him —

(*Say, love, if you are listening,
is there anything you need?*)

Isaiah Vianese

DRINKING SONG

Give me a body to hold tonight,
light, a sip, some song to sing

to bring you home again —

baby, put something bright
to my lips, if this tune calls you in.

LOVE, AGAIN

Baby, let's narcotize ourselves
with sex, put on some Bronski Beat
and rock the night away.

Face it: I'm a small town boy
with the same old stories to tell — stories
someone has already told.

We can pretend we believe
in love, place bets on length or duration.
No. We shouldn't pretend at all —

love's just the song the drag queen
can only lip-synch, not sing,
a blinking neon sign, the last drop of gin.

Let's drive some old road, invite
each other in, sing some good news —
the stars have blues enough.

SURRENDER

Walking home at night, a man
followed me for a long time.
Pulling the scarf to my face,
I hustled, worried about my gait
being too gentle, worried
about wearing my tightest jeans.
He kept my pace, flustered
that I hurried, the wind spitting darkness.
The street lamps seemed dim —
Matthew Shepherd tied to a fence again —
and I lamented moving to this city,
this wash of mini-malls and frat houses.
Then he turned down another street,
maybe trailing me by accident,
maybe just giving up.

EASY RIDER

My brother got his motorcycle license.
Now he will know what it feels like
to ride something with power.
After my boyfriend and I broke up, we still
had sex. He liked to pin my arms down
while he was above me.

Sometimes, he would let me be on top,
and I enjoyed the hunger
to make him do what I wanted,
but he outweighed me by thirty pounds,
could buck me off, bruise me, take my life
if he wanted to, or if I asked.

Too many jokes have been made about lovers
and automobiles — *easy rider*, if I recall —
but I should tell my brother,
when I refuse to drive his bike,
I know danger, understand adoring
what can break you at any moment.

A YEAR IS A LONG TIME

There have been other things: the garden
and its endless wanting, the old dog
asking for food, a walk, to pee in the yard.
I'm trying to say I haven't had a date in a while.

I haven't read so many books lately,
though I think about it.
I haven't written as much as I'd like to say.
I've made too many meals from a box.

My old boyfriend has someone new. He's settled
down. I mean I don't need things settled.
Someone could toss me up a little. A year
is a long time. I've done my share of longing.

TONIGHT, A SWEET NOSTALGIA

The waiter said *I think I remember you.*
We ordered what we used to when
we were together — some eel in sauce
and avocado sushi with cream cheese.

The talk included books, of course,
and how some music album was not quite
what we hoped — a little sloppy.

You looked fabulous bringing the teacup
to your lips, sipping, wearing a new hat.
I loved you again, like I did once,
and for a moment, when I touched
your hand, you smiled into that old tune too.

MADDEN
ED

burning fields

Ed Madden was born and raised in rural Arkansas. His first book of poetry, *Signals,* was winner of the South Carolina Poetry Book Prize, selected by Afaa Weaver. His work appears in *Best New Poets 2007* and *The Book of Irish American Poetry from the Eighteenth Century to the Present.* He is also the author of *Tiresian Poetics,* a study of modernist poetry, and co-editor of *Out Loud: The Best of Rainbow Radio,* a collection of radio essays from one of the only gay and lesbian radio programs in the South. His second book of poetry, *Prodigal: Variations,* was recently published, and a third book, *Nest,* is forthcoming. He is also the writer in residence for the Riverbanks Botanical Gardens in Columbia, South Carolina. He teaches at the University of South Carolina.

FOR WHAT I ASSUME IS MEMBERSHIP

That was the first party, and all those bodies stippling the carpet,
whispers about a military man, out of uniform, and below us

the dark trails. He touched me on the balcony, asked me if
we could keep each other's secrets — the parsing of all those lies.

The car wouldn't start, I said, or was it the *too-late-to-drive* story?

Later there was that yellow letter, some drivel about love,
a rug, a key to a trunk full of porn, and something about *if I die*.

I told the man from the laundry about it, after he folded his clothes
and we traded massage in a room filled with steam — like any story,

another clunky fiction of seduction. But that was months later.
We leaned on the balcony then, naked, below us the lake's edge

in ruffles of black, bats stitching the dark air, men
on moon-dark paths below, following a sound too fine to hear,

the way my first love turned that day, as if — turned at the corner,
turned and waited.

DREAM FATHERS

We drive across the bridge, late at night,
a hundred feet or so of clattering boards —

no rail, no rim, just jagged planks, and river
flowing slow and brown below. The bridge

collapsed last year. I cross it every night
in sleep — sometimes alone, sometimes with him —

but always *away* from home. The bridge's end
may veer; each night I go someplace else,

dark cypress swamp on either side.
One night my father is the driver and the car.

He opens up the door of his side,
and I climb in. I cross the bridge again,

riding in the body of my father.

*

In the dream, the road is never straight. Fear
seizes my heart. A woman who doesn't see me

is there, and a man shouting the name of someone
lost or dead. He will beg me to come

to him, he will plead, and he will take me
in his bloody arms — he will destroy me.

A dark man stands beside the bed,
the hair on his chest glistens, nipples I want

to suck — like shame from my father's breast.

Another man lies in bed beside me.
His hands aren't bloody; he's not my father.

We are what we are.

*

In the darkness, he whispers names for shame
like magic charms. I turn to him, drawn

by hard arms, the heat of dark eyes.
A snakebite scars his hand, exactly where

a cottonmouth bit my father as a child.
He almost died. The man slices open

his left breast, the hinge of skin peeled
back to expose the heart. He lifts it out,

he kisses it as if he were the one who broke it —
blood on his lips, blood and cum on mine.

My father says he doesn't understand
a man who'd sleep with other men.

Almost every night I sleep with him.

PLAYGROUND

When Mark Nicholson spilled his milk on me — a slosh
across my lap — the teacher let me tip the rest
on him, then slipped me in some spare jeans in her closet,
and that was that. From then on, *teacher's pet.*

Carroll Toddy fell out the back of a swing that fall,
knocked him out, left a knot on his round head
like a horn. On cold days, our teams devolved
to backwards tag, the boy with the ball running the field,

and all the rest after him — *smear the queer* — trying
to tag or tackle him. No way to win. Tagged, he'd toss
the ball, lob it in the mob of us, or hurl it high —
snag it and *you're it* — scramble past, run cross

the yard. No out of bounds, no teams, no rules,
until the bell called us back inside for school.

JUBILATE

For I will read queer things in punk magazines in English.
For we will talk about David Bowie and Rod Stewart in art.
For I will watch Sting sing 'Don't stand so close to me' on *Friday Night Videos*
as I lie on a bed in Sheryl Honey's house my senior year,
for I will lie on the bed with Elizabeth, who loaned me the magazines,
for I will lie on the bed with Paul, the quarterback with perfect hair and
tanned ankles, for we will watch Sting sing 'Don't stand so close to me.'

Let us rejoice with Rod Stewart, who says
no point in talking when there's nobody listening.
Let us rejoice with Sting, who sings,
don't stand so, don't stand, don't stand.
Copa Cabana, Mama Mia, Amen.

For there is a bar in Oxford called the Jolly Farmer.
Thou knowest my downsitting and mine uprising,
thou understandest my thought afar off.
For there I will meet a man named David,
for we will hear the Pet Shop Boys sing, 'Take a chance on me.'
Such knowledge is too wonderful for me –
For we will wait in line to enter Heaven, where I will dance with David –
If I ascend up into heaven, thou art there –
for I will hear a remix of 'Even better than the real thing'
and we will leave together –
if I make my bed in hell, behold thou art there.

For what you do when you are confused
will make you certain.

Ed Madden

ABOUT THE ROOM IN WHICH

I

About the room in which it first happened,
I remember little, beyond a man

named Ron who offered a soda, then led me
to a room with a bed, said

he thought I'd find *The Joy of Gay Sex*
a useful intro to what men sometimes do.

I did. The book was heavy as his hand
in my lap, as I scanned the pages —

and after, as I drove away.

II

A walk-in closet, three boys, and the enigma
of sex — a father's magazine, and what it

could do to them, what it did. No script,
but stripped, pajamas under pillows, they played

a strange game of guy and gal — and then
a reporter snapping scandal, joining in.

Where'd we learn these things, and why do they
now return? The closet was in a house

that later burned.

III

About Larry's house, three rooms,
but first the dirt, those jars of soil and sand —

lands he'd traveled lining the den, and when
we began, and it was clear that this was

where and when, I dropped my contacts in two
cups on the kitchen counter. Later,

I woke in the warm dark, sure I'd heard
the last trumpets, sure that Christ had found me

there — naked, jittery, and spent.

PRODIGAL: VARIATIONS

And he said, A certain man had two sons...

Plowing beans takes concentration. Line up the plow
in the long green rows — position the left wheel's axle bolt

directly above a row and watch the wheel whir the furrow,
or put the hood's chrome-figured tip between two rows

the tractor straddles — these necessary, inaccurate alignments.
My brother was better than me at the plow. I remember

the difficult turns, remember the dark soil, the bright blades,
my father waiting at the other end.

*

A man watches the road.
He will see me coming.

Even a great way off, he will see me coming.

*

Sometimes harvest went on into dark —
wives unwrapping sandwiches in wax paper,

men eating off the tailgates of old trucks.
I sat in the back, watching them eat,

handed my dad the thermos of coffee.
Soon, my brother would demand to join

the men in the fields. I never did.
The lights of the combines combed the field.

*

A *certain man had two sons*. What is he certain of?

*

I read the forecast, think of the garden —
the last tomatoes, the garlic.

I do not think of my father on a narrow bed.

I have a cigar box filled with sacred objects:
clay marble, paper badge, white ribbon, bone.

*

Was it death?
Or a scar hardening across the heart?

Was it death?
Or just the silence left behind?

I look at the sealed letter in my hand,
drop it in the drawer with all the others.

*

There were fields on fire, the way they used to burn
the stubble, starting over for the cotton, starting over

for the sorghum and the beans, starting fresh.

I remember the acrid smell of the burning fields,
a grassy soot, the porch covered in black dust.

*

He spills his love, pours it out.
The residue sticks to skin like shame.

The air is filled with fire and ash.
The past is a field filled with flame.

A man had two sons:
footprints in the black pollen on the porch.

*

This is not a sty.
This is not my father's house.
These are not the cities of the plain.

You find the thing you need.
I tell myself, A certain man had two sons....

*

A certain man had two sons.

They are the empty chairs at the table.

They are the dust on the bedpost.

They are the scar on the brow.

KNOWLEDGE
Dublin, May 2006

I.

On the schoolboy's list, the GPO, famed portico,
this row of six stone columns — we check it off, done —

Cuchulain and the crow in the window, then the spire —
the stiffie at the *Liffey* someone says — Parnell, our Joyce

jaunty boyo in a nearby street. Later, after dinner,
I wander back on my own, finger the fluted columns'

grooves, the nicks and knocks, bulleted pocks.

II.

We walked the path up Knocknarea — that knuckle
of rock — a rutted lane dissolving to a trail

over stone and heather, shudder of sheep gates, drizzle
pelting the top. All the way down we named the flowers —

orchid, pennywort, furze, vetch. The rain
came harder. In walls of rock along the bottom lane,

clumps of primrose glowed between the stones.

III.

A few years back, I met a Wexford gardener in Temple Bar —
shy smile and thick hair, a spurt of it flirting his collar, and,

I'd discover, a filigree of jet on his chest, insular script
embellishing each nip and the rest — *his heart was going like mad* —

mouth sweet with beer and sweat, hard hips in hands,
and in the dark, the shiver and stiffness, the brogue and braille

of him — each sweet bud, each cleft, traced with finger, tongue.

TERRY
DANIEL NATHAN

false resurrection

Daniel Nathan Terry was the recipient of the 2007 Stevens Poetry Manuscript Award for his first full-length collection, *Capturing the Dead*, which was published in 2008. His chapbook, *Waxwings*, was a finalist for the Robin Becker Prize and was published in July of 2010 by Seven Kitchens Press. His latest chapbook, *Days of Dark Miracles*, is from the same press. His poetry has appeared or is forthcoming in several literary journals including *Poet Lore, Naugatuck River, New South* and *The MacGuffin*. He received an MFA in Creative Writing from UNC-Wilmington in May of 2010.

SCARECROW

Scarecrow crafter, burlap-tailor,
black-eye smudger, when I'm done,
crows mistake you for a man:
silent shooer, stock-still farmer,
to them alone a tartan terror.
I fisted through your flannel,
spiced your straw with artemesia,
puffed your chest with wilted-rue,
perfumed your thighs with summer sweet —
another half-attempt at love — and to keep
the flies from you, who do not care
if you are flesh or straw; stand still in June,
they will devour you. If they don't and you see
the summer through, the sun, the wind, the rain
make fast work of you until your pie-pan hands
cease to flutter and the crows
begin to mutter that you can't be much.
Winter comes, now the squash begins
to earn its name, cold snaps beans.
Like tomatoes that turn from green to glass
my red for you is missing.
How long before the snow and I
take you down?

SELF-PORTRAIT (GAY SON OF A PREACHER)

Old enough for evening service,
too young to stay awake, for a moment the boy
sleeps against his mother's side,

his left hand clutching the pale green hem
of her blouse. He wakes suddenly,
falling, a rush downward, a startling sureness

of his own destruction, his little soul
trailing his body like a failed parachute.
His father's voice opens in the waking world.

It is the voice of Jesus — deep as a baptistery.
The sermon is halfway over,
but the boy hears enough — Naaman,

once a great warrior, became a Leper,
ghost-white, his flesh a torn garment
of wounds. And he remained that way —

until he obeyed God's prophet, washed
seven times in the river Jordan and his flesh
was made clean and new as a child's.

The boy's fear slips away — he releases
his mother. He rises, joins the altar call.
His father's arms open

before him, wafer and wine in his hands,
the congregation sings *Just as I Am.*
But the boy, silent, mouth open,

hears only his Savior — a voice
in his chest — saying *Come,*
and I will make you whole.

POWDER-BLUE BROTHER

Bunk-beds were windows,
when you were on the bottom

and your brother left the top
to take his midnight piss. You saw

him slip from the upper,
the soles of his feet, his legs,

then all the rest. When he touched
down his body quivered.

When he returned, you noticed
for the first time, with only the moon

for light, the room was blue.
He walked toward you. One hand

soothed an itch. His cock descended
in your direction, lowered

with each sleepy step. Reaching
the bed, he paused, inches away. All

you saw of him was nipples to knees.
His thigh muscles tensed. Then

he pulled himself up and out
of your sight and you were left alone.

RED HORSE

Most nights, the boy grooms the red horse.
Most days the boy re-bags the trash
in the cinderblock pit by the road.

Both have to be done so he doesn't complain,
though the horse is a only dream, and the pit is his
town's way of dealing with trash.

His true nature is beautiful — a long-necked statue
precariously left on the picnic table. One night
while strapping the mane of the red horse,

the boy sees the statue tip and fall from the table.
There is a hairline crack from chin to sternum.
He uprights it again, more carefully, but still

he is broken. The red horse will never forgive him.
Weeks pass before the town sends its trucks
to the country. In that time the rain

and sun melt the black plastic and the trash
festers, is riddled with maggots. The boy
takes up his shovel and five new bags,

prays he will unearth the broken statue
in the pit. There is a neighbor boy who is older — he waits
on the back porch swing, his cock is always hard.

Some nights, some days, the boys groom each other
when the red horse won't come or when the cropduster
does and the fields by the road are unsafe. Sometimes

the cropduster half-moons over the porch, nearly stalls,
engine like a chainsaw as it turns back to the melon fields.
Another pass. The stench is all over them

now. The red horse can't always be returned to.
The broken statue never returns. The boy
with the shovel no longer digs for it.

CALLED COLORED, IN MY YOUTH,
for Tyrell Jenkins, 1966-1991

they picked cucumbers in the fields around our house —
large, dark women squatted on downturned buckets
to bring the ground nearer their hands, to rest their knees.

Boys my age who should have been in school worked beside them,
paid by the bucket, shirtless and black as their mothers' brows. Afternoons,
I watched from the porch swing — the boys' slim bodies bent at the waist,

their jeans riding low on brown hips. Now and again
I was blessed with a glimpse of smooth skin that I knew
was forbidden. The Gaddys, who owned the fields,

called them *niggers*, but my mother allowed them
the use of our bathroom. The neighborhood trashed
us, said we were dirty and that they'd never touch a thing

in our house. Called us *Nigger-lovers*, said *the blackness comes off*.
Warned me not to play with the colored boys or I'd get mine.
I already knew I shouldn't want to play with those boys, shouldn't

want boys of any color the way I wanted the oldest of them — Tyrell,
fifteen, the one Miss Gaddy spat was *so black he's blue*. Tyrell
who looked like the David I conjured when my father read from the Bible.

But that near-holiness didn't stay my hardness, didn't close my mouth
as I watched him sweat and bend. I wanted to touch Tyrell, wanted
to feel the hot night I believed he carried on his back,

wanted to take him in my hand, my mouth, wanted
to find out for myself if the blackness would really come
off on my pink skin. So I did, and in some way, it did. One day

I heard screams — a copperhead, long as a broom and thick as man's
wrist found coiled beneath the umbrellas of the long cucumber vines.
Tyrell, who I believed by then I loved, rushed

to where his mother pointed while the others ran
from the field. With one iron arc of his right arm, he sliced
the snake's head off with a machete, then tossed the writhing,

bloody rope into the roadside ditch beside our house.
Days later, after I heard he'd been arrested for stealing a car,
I walked to the ditch to see my champion's kill.

Headless, it seemed alive, its body still undulating
like the sea lived inside its brown and pink skin, bucked the way I did
some nights when I came, when I woke with the dark night

dreams across my belly. A closer look exposed this false resurrection —
from the wound in its neck, I could see maggots hollowing
its body. The snake was dead, but thousands of little white lives

wouldn't let it rest.

SINCE THEY PUT YOU OUT

no chair receives you,
no bath invites you,
no stove pot simmers
you to supper, no mattress
gives to cradle you,
no down rises to fill
the empty spaces
your spine leaves behind
in the back-bending nightmares
you've suffered since
you got the shove. Since
you got the boot, no door
thuds protectively behind you,
no hallway echoes
without reminding you,
your feet fall too much
alone. Since they kicked you
to the curb, no memory
of mama makes you warm,
no papa's chestnut
is worth the recollection
of Sammy cracking your tooth
in the seventh grade
because you were too pretty,
too soft, too much for him —
what you did for him behind
the shed. This made the journey
from home to hell not easier,
but expected. Like a whore
you know love turns
on a dime.

NIGHTHAWKS

Nighthawks boomerang through the haloes
of streetlamps, skimming so close to the blacktop
a leaping child could catch one by its narrow wings

and hurl it back into the blackness. From the front steps,
the young man watches them dive in and out of the night,
beaks wide, sifting insects from the humid air. A pickup

rumbles down the street. In its wake, the nighthawks lift
and scatter like long leaves, then whirlwind
back to business. A mosquito

lights on the young man's temple, its legs soft and black
as eyelashes — then the sharp bite, blood stolen,
poison deposited — his reflexive slap too slow

to accomplish anything but crushing the miracle.
A knot rises beneath his skin which he will scratch
tomorrow like regret. His taxi arrives,

its low beams thick with life. At his feet lantana thrums
with nocturnal moths gathering nectar, escaping the feeding frenzy
in the waves of electric light, but opening themselves

to the skinks and spiders that lurk in the brambles. Bar cash
and condoms tucked in his back pocket, he walks
toward the cab as nature struggles with the equation —

comings minus goings, feathers divided by proboscises,
stars multiplied by the number of open eyes —
the sum of his need hanging in the balance.

HARKER
JOSEPH

dare me to love this rubble

Joseph Harker is the pseudonym of a twentysomething raising hell up and down the East Coast of America. Between jobs and cities, he has nothing better to do than write poems, go clubbing, and point out the beautiful sunsets. You can find his work in journals such as *Qarrtsiluni*, *Chantarelle's Notebook*, and *Ganymede*. Some day in the near future, he'll finally put together a chapbook or something.

http://namingconstellations.wordpress.com

TASTING

Some say it improves with age, but to tell the truth,
I never cared much for those vintages:
too much like mushroom salad two days too old,
laced with the note of cigarettes if he's a smoker
or the weak sweetness of the beer
that got you both into this in the first place.
There are recipes to it
as with any other rarefied vice. Balanced diet,
vegetarian if possible. Plenty of tropical fruits, tofu and
leafy greens. Healthy lifestyle and water
and salt. No air pollution.
I had a twenty-six-year-old Valencian once,
punctuated with the breath of sea spray.
A twenty-year Chesapeake like lemongrass
and oregano. And the '75 Zanzibar
thick with fire, full of soil and steam. Spit out my title
like it's a bad thing, but to each his own, and I will
talk about bouquets and body as easily as
any sommelier. Those champagne splits are best
wrapped in denim and buttons:
remember to be selective, and to let yourself breathe.

METRO BOYS

Metro boys,
you tempt me into railway affairs.
I'd like to clack my glasses up against yours,
and feel that perfectly-groomed stubble graze my cheek.
I'd like to bury my nose in the flesh of your neck,
suffocate myself in your bath and body shop scent,
invite that moisturized couture to line my lungs.
I'd like to tear at your mall-sale jewelry,
so carefully chosen and deliberated, returned and recaptured,
to match the sparkle in your hazelnut eyes,
or the gleam of your straightened canines.
I'd like to stop the train and spend some rhythm with you.

Metro boys,
thank God for your ignorance,
tended like an orchid with years of pretense.
I must cross my legs when you sigh like an angel
about philosophy class or credit card limits,
the old fart boss in his thirties or the scuff mark of your boot.
I must time my vibrations with the train's to avoid
embarrassing myself at the cosmopolitan lies of your names.
I must hold myself back when your manicured hands
run through coiffed hair and pick fuzz from your slacks,
every action rehearsed and chosen from thousands.
I'd like to be your equal and opposite reaction.

Metro boys,
drama is not the way we move.
It's only a bad day when the doors finally hiss open
and you carry on like swans into the good part of town,
away from me. Metro boys,
miss your stop.

BOY. FIFTY DOLLARS.

I paid him cash, but only just to talk
and tell of how he fell into this fate,
all curbside-sale and jangly tight-jean walk.

With no one out on Market Street this late,
he tells of how he fell into this fate,
thrown out, no shoes, the day he turned fifteen

with no one, out on Market Street, quite late.
He names the shelter where he'd first been seen:
thrown out, no shoes, the day he turned fifteen

(his father caught him, beat him, chased him out).
He names the shelter where he'd first been seen,
where men, in whispers, soothed despair and doubt.

"Your father caught you, beat you, chased you out?
Come walk with us, lay down that troubled head."
The men, in whispers, soothed despair and doubt.

And better that than end up raped and dead.
He walked with them, laid down his troubled head,
wrapped up in arms and legs that pushed and thrust

(but better that than end up raped and dead),
cried out the first few times, but learned to trust
the men whose arms and legs would push and thrust

his body out in unforgiving night.
Cried out the first few weeks, but learned to trust
the other boys on pavement, cool and white.

His body sold to unforgiving night,
to touch its face and slowly fade away,
like other boys on pavement, cool and white

he told himself, it's business anyway.
He touched my face and turned to fade away,
so curbside-sale and jangly tight-jean walk.

I told myself, it's business anyway.
I paid him cash. But only just to talk.

AMSTERDAM

He ran California marathons, and it showed,
lithe body made more scandalous by clothes
too thin for the seaborne summer evening.

Downstairs they had a Scandinavian god
stripped naked and flexing like a sidewinder.
On either side were mirrors, just in case

we forgot to admire him, and he had to
finish himself off. Upstairs the labyrinth,
black-velvet-curtained and candle-flamed

occupied by heavy businessman shadows
and tourist twinks, mustachioed leathermen,
a distance runner with four drinks too many

and me. Exhibitionism caught me with
my pants down: his eyes, so used to the
sprint of air along the 101, screwed closed;

his smooth lips were caught in a long O.
Through the curtain only I saw them all at once,
any of them older than me by half and more

and I felt just like a Scandinavian god,
pornographically beautiful, for fifteen
poorly-lit minutes, until our scene was over

and we stepped out into a brackish night.
He talked too loudly about philosophy
and love, pausing only to piss in the gutter.

REPTILE

Improbable,
that one animal should wear so much leather at once
so comfortably,
great tectonic sheets of it
dully gleaming against your pale hairless skin.

Perhaps
if those lips were not so thin and wide in their bow,
or sclera and iris could be discerned behind those shades,
journeying from one stop to the next
would not seem so long.

Instead,
the hum of the track becomes a low, lustful moan
and the tap of metal the sharp smack of a gloved hand
that now curls perversely paternal
around the chrome-plated poles.

So
the trance is uneasily broken
when you descend, combat boots thumping the platform
in search of more well-oiled gentlemen,
Komodo dragon seeking its squirming prey.

WHY WE CAN'T GET MARRIED YET

Because you live a thousand miles away where the winters
    lie leaden over the lakes, snow whispering like crepe paper.
Because it's only legal in six states and nine countries where you won't go
    and if I crash my car in Virginia they won't even let you in.
Because your glass-bottom flights to Malibu and Bombay
    leave every evening and carry who I thought you were away.
Because I am young, and you are young, and the world is young,
    and there are so many boys still out there to sleep with.
Because a white tuxedo would hang off of my shoulders like a shroud,
    dull church bells in our ears a counterpoint to a musty old organ.
Because you want so little, so much, and I want so little, so much,
    and sometimes it's hard to tell who's being kinder to whom.
Because I still don't know, after all these years, if you are in fact
    Mister Right, Prince Charming, and The One all at once.
Because deep down, neither of us is brave enough to admit
    that we are afraid of what goes on when the other slips out of sight.

QUEER

When I passed you in the men's room, and your eyes took in
the tongue ring, pipelegged jeans, pink hair and perfect nails,
I loved how you murmured "faggot" like a prayer,
so much more reverent than "cocksucker",
"homo" or "fairy", coming from you,
in your sweat stained overalls and
Confederate cap, although
next time, stranger, will be
better for us both
if you say it
and look me
in the
eye.

MOTHER LILITH

you vanished into history, but still
i've seen you, mother Lilith, in the night:
on bleecker street, your maquillage divine,
in darkened saunas, steaming through the night,
on stage, the curtains rising with your glory,
and under bridges, shy and wrapped with night;

before the fall, your rhythm was your own,
you countered yang with yin, and day with night,
and Lilith meant uniquely beautiful,
as indescribable as star-struck night,
your children are the ones who think and act,
who share their indiscretions in the night;

the prostitutes, the pierced-tongue boys, the queens,
the leather crowd, the ones who move at night:
you've left your independent DNA
in all our bloodstreams, subtle as the night,
your evolutionary stride is long,
and pulses with the humming of the night;

you spread your ancient wings and spiraled up,
beyond the indigo that heralds night,
and left a million triumphs here to touch,
to break taboos, to populate the night:
but mother Lilith, fabulous and bright,
without your face, how lonely is the night;

with love, i pray that queer and shapely light
reveals itself, and banishes the night.

EHAB (THE STRIPPER'S TALE)

Some fierce deity has got his hooks in, dangling his progeny
from invisible strings looped through holes down that supple spine,
making motions that no boy could ever hope
to accomplish on his own:

when the Red Sea was parted, or when the muscles
in Jacob's arms tensed as he wrestled with the angel,
when the little swallows of fire descended in peals of unearthly breath,
all of it was curvilinear, following contours of motion
that match the golden mean, that are supernatural in their beauty,
and now we see them here, on a dimly dirty stage:

we see the flower of the East, stubble beginning on his cheeks
and his chest, the careful caramel of his skin, and those limbs,
feline and liquid, panther of the dappled jungle
turned man, and presented here for the other men to admire:

still, what a zoo it is when he gets up for the twelve-o-clock set,
black Speedo and sneakers and nothing more,
feeling the tugs of a heavenly hand running down to hip and shoulder,
gyrating him until he is no longer the dancer but the steps of the dance,
the expression of some greater artistry making itself known
through the manipulation of form:

and yet when he closes his eyes and the daddies stick sweaty dollars
down the front of his waistband, letting their hands linger too long,
it takes a brilliance that is entirely human to resist
and to remember he is paid to be explored.

SONNET FOR ZACHARY

They wouldn't let him say the Kaddish,
Gentile as he was. Their muffled weeping echoed
through the room. He saw the small corrections
they had made, as though
they could pretend their prince's lesions weren't there,
his wasted body an illusion. Afterward, the parents
headed home without a word to the
impostor lover, he who tasted their son's skin
before it turned to ash. But he is sitting shiva:
he is covering the mirrors, closing windows,
goy performing rites and
trying not to gnash his teeth.
He'll be all right, he thinks. In love, is strength.
He lights a candle for the boy.

BISMILLAH

The war wrecked the foundations of sleep:
so now your nights are spent at the drafting table,
mechanical pencils wielded like a pair of rapiers
tattooing the page, while chemical magic
swims your sleepless bloodstream.
But I've seen how you dream: how often I've wiped
a sweat-stained brow furrowed so completely
while demon-voiced firecrackers are going off
through all the dusty streets in your past.
The derelict houses, shutters shut, sunlight
in their bulletholes showing glowing curtains
of stone and plaster dust.

I've seen the angles in your calligraphic circlets,
the jagged points jutting out from the whorls,
a dozen elbows from a perfectly deformed body
whose shape is forbidden save in letters.
You wrote my portrait once: I unfolded thin
and thorned, vowels dangling from my chin,
cobalt shading of your pen following parallel lines
that broke and rejoined. (For so much in us
has done the same.) When your eyelids slide over
those oil slick infinities, and your lips part
with the names of God, I can see your accent marks.

I can see the night I took your virginity spelled out,
geometric and trembling. I can see you in His Image.

But we cannot look round the corners of memory's
snaking pathways. Your mother's faithful disgust,
your brother's shamefaced pity. If God is the
All-Compassionate, tell me why this rout, this final
attrition on a body that has suffered so much.
Perhaps that's why it's drawn sharp at the edges
while chestnut skin and its sparse blanket of coal hair
are so soft. You defy these disasters as stubbornly
as broken glass. You dare me to love this rubble,
lie down with what strength is found in destruction.

You wrote a self-portrait once:
it arced piecemeal and proud, and no shame
blinked behind the consonants of your eyes.

JACQUES
ROB

don't tell the guys

Rob Jacques grew up in northern New England. He served in the U.S. Navy during the Vietnam Era, and while on a tour of duty as an officer-instructor at the U.S. Naval Academy, he met his partner (a fellow officer) of 37 years. He has taught technical writing at the college level, and his poetry has appeared in numerous literary journals. He currently resides on Bainbridge Island in Washington State's Puget Sound.

ARTIST'S MODEL
for Vincent

Advanced class on the human form
stands ready to create in the art lab
with easels prepared, canvas spread,
oils, palettes and brushes at the ready,
students suitably studious, serious,
instructor waiting while the last cap
on the last paint tube is removed.

A lanky grasshopper of a nude boy,
stern-faced, bubble-assed, feet too big,
all lengthy thighs and long shin bones,
steps matter-of-factly, nonchalantly
from behind a screen to an artistic pose,
those raw-boned long legs awkward,
still not under a gawky youth's control.

And he will be drawn, not as he is,
but as he is seen, the artists' art being
to bring to be just what is being done
in their brains, done with endorphins,
serotonins, dopamine, hormones
tweaking fibrous strains of gray matter
into recreating lean Adam in Eden.

A woman, motherly, fleshes him out.
A man, fatherly, paints the waist up.
A girl, shy, goes cubist, fat squares.
But one boy blushes, yearns for him,
palette-knifes his passion thickly,
summoning courage (spoils going
to those who dare) to ask him out.

But the gawky, raw-boned boy, bare,
puts his mind in neutral as he sits
long-legged with big feet, unaware
he's inert ore fondled by imaginations,
artists frigging with reality to create
offspring out of temptation and dirt
lovelier by far than any reasoned thing.

I ASKED HIS STORY

> *I asked his story. It's the same story.*
> *Every story the same story no matter what's said,*
> *by whom, any gender it doesn't matter*
> *because why never changes.*
>
> Raymond Taylor

I think in a week I won't remember him,
even in a day recall his face, a bit older
than it had appeared in last night's dark bar,
his cock no longer swollen, having done
its job shooting his wad down my throat.

The chaste clock on the cheap nightstand
says now what it wouldn't say last night
(telling time in the midst of our sexual run)
but there's time for small talk to be polite,
not rush off as if the sex hadn't been fun,

and so I listen. He's me, you, all of us,
saying what you and I and all would say.
Much is de rigueur and much pro forma,
and he pauses at appropriate places for
my "Hmm," "Really!" and "I understand."

But it's such repetition, my having heard
eagles crying the same thing from aeries,
having read Sophocles, having lived Proust,
having, as a slick teen, jacked myself raw
like the solipsistic Pre-Raphaelite poets.

When he asks for my story, I'm bored
and say, "It's the same basic plot as yours,
which is why we're here, you and I,
for a one-time exchange of bodily fluids
where, for once, we don't fear the dark."

Later, all I remember of him is me. You.
All of the fucking, spoiled human race.
I recall our story with tinselly grace and rue,
the merciless gods and soiled playthings
that damn us all, all of us false and true.

Rob Jacques

MUSIC BOX DANCER ON A MUSIC BOX FOR A BOY

Let's get one thing straight right away:
I'm an action figure, not a doll,
and I'm moving to martial music,
not ballet. See my uniform?
It's not a costume. See my baton?
It's not a wand. I'm lithe, young,
athletic as hell with buttocks to die for.

My steps are more precision drill
than a girly mince or pirouette,
and though I'm hot and fleet of foot,
make no mistake: my force is brute
and more toward BSDM than not.
My music box holds coins, not rings;
bones and stones and curious things.

Dad feels comfortable with me,
my overt masculinity, while Mom
adores my rousing shape and shine,
and their maturing boy likes me, too,
plays with me, mimics my sublime
turning, eyes of an eagle, not a dove,
with me, their boy awakening to love.

Dad feels comfortable with me,
my overt masculinity, while Mom
adores my rousing shape and shine,
and their maturing boy likes me, too,
plays with me, mimics my sublime
turning, eyes of an eagle, not a dove,
with me, their boy awakening to love.

RADIO FLYER

Pulling my red wagon, white-wheeled,
clean, black-handled and rubber-tired,
I saw him smooth and slender sitting
on his doorstep like a boyish Achilles
awaiting Patroclus at the gates of Troy,
his dark hair unkempt, his large eyes
robin's-egg blue watching my approach.

I'd felt funny looking at other boys
at recess or in class a few desks away,
felt strange rainbows, skipping thrills,
but this one awoke a fierce hollowness,
my voice catching, my mouth dry,
my knees weak, and I fought to be me:
normal, casual, quiet, my life a lie

this boy would like. This boy would
want. So it was I wheeled my wagon
to his feet, stopped, and fell hard under
the bright spotlight of his dimpled smile.
"Wanna go for a ride? Make my body
be your horse?" and his head cocked
to one side. He considered the course

this event would take, this beginning,
this introduction to meeting feelings
head on. And he slowly got up, got in
while my heart beat hard and I steadied
the wagon better than I steadied myself.
I pulled while looking back at him
watching me with that moist smile.

At no time since have I pulled treasure
greater than that boy. I was proud.
I was awake and aware for the first time
of what I was, my soup of hormones
crying out loud, my testosterone amok,
screaming "To hell with everything
that isn't this beautiful, attainable boy!"

My red wagon held a pretty Hermes,
was a chariot hauling my pubertal Eros,
was the lone vehicle I've had that held
what God most loved: His own Adam.
I turned at the end of a too-short street,
even as I calculated how on sweet earth
I could fix it so our lips would meet.

And when I'd returned him safely,
I knelt beside him, leaned toward him,
whispering, "My Mom says a boy, if he
really likes him, can give another boy
a kiss." Slowly, softly, our wet lips met.
Was this what my minister meant when
he talked of a loving God's gift of bliss?

WATER TOWER

"Jesus!" football-hero Billy said, "It's far down,"
his big, blue eyes even bigger, his innocence
frightening him, a boy at the top of everything
that matters, a boy I'd have kissed in a heartbeat.

Night hid us, camouflaged our paint-party climb,
"Class of '09" on our minds, letters high and tight,
we, the latest in a long line of senior volunteers
spraying annual immortal graffiti by flashlight.

Billy was fine on flat, striped fields, in his element
in a fast car on a back road with an adoring crowd,
Billy the star in the backseat with petty, pretty girls,
Billy as self-assured as he was lovely and endowed.

But one hundred fifty feet up dew-slicked steel,
one hundred fifty feet up on a cold, slight slant
that slipped away more and more until sudden plunge,
one hundred fifty feet up made him sweat, pant,

and I was surprised. He was cute, so wide-eyed
and shivering attractively with fright. Who knew?
Who knew his acrophobia would be my friend?
"I can't do this," was his girlish, quavering wail.

"Of course you can," I smiled, inching closer
to where he sat frozen in his neurotic fear of falling.
"Take my hand." He quickly grabbed mine, held on
as if something precious depended on our mutual grip

and I felt his wet, erotic clamminess, his cold sweat
rousing me to a feat of daring equal to a touchdown
as I slipped my arm around him, hugged him to me,
Billy obeying my tug of sexually charged protection.

"Don't leave me here," he whispered hoarsely, and
he needn't have feared, my feeling his muscular heft,
smooth, sweaty hand, sweet breath from that beer
he'd had, all combining to keep us coupled, close.

"Don't tell the guys," he whispered as we heard
their car radios far, far below, and his lovely eyes
pleaded for mercy. "I'll be right back," I sighed,
loath to let go of buxom Billy's body and hand,

but I slid legs-first to the far edge, to just before
a slight, insipient slant became a certain-death fall.
I spray-painted high-school glory in glimmer-gold,
moving over slowly, carefully, testosterone-bold.

And when I'd finished and was back beside him,
he nervously took my hand again and squeezed
while I leaned forward. "You owe me this," and
I kissed his wet lips, my flesh aroused, pleased.

"Don't tell the guys," he said as I kissed him more,
finally helping him move to handle the steel bar
that would guide him down one hundred fifty feet
to his many high school buddies, still their star.

TAB HUNTER

In the dark, I watched harmlessly, transfixed without fear
of who was watching me. Safely relaxed, I disappeared,
free to experience puppy love so forbidden even now I gulp
in my amazement at daring back then, back when at fourteen
in the dark, I longed to make my two-dimensional love for you
a three-dimensional sin. Your beauty took me in when I ached
to be touched by an understanding that transcends damnation.
In the dark theater of my frightened mind, on my own silver screen,
I projected in the dark behind my eyes scenes Mom and Dad
should never see, re-running hot pleasure with an embodied god.
Backwards and forwards, I re-ran you perfectly, always secretly,
always masking my desire for your unbelievable loveliness,
I, bashful, masking my closeted ways when nice-looking boys
made me catch my breath. My heart took flight even as I longed
for death. My only joy was in the dark where fiction played
better than common sense, where on an immense screen people
sang and loved and danced unafraid in the dark and meant it.

You were real, you were true. You sought girls unabashed
in your brilliant flesh, your smiling desire obvious to Sophia, Rita,
Natalie, Lana, Debbie and Kim and even Divine. I hurt in the dark
at your every kiss. Why couldn't I be like you and live in bliss?
Why couldn't I like girls, too? In the dark, why did I pine for boys
when boys pined for girls you so easily kissed, so easily romanced
from the first reel through the last? Successful flirt, you made girls
feel worthy of you while in the dark, I died. My bed in the dark
was an island of aching that couldn't be reached by those I loved
in the solitary confinement of myself. In the dark, I dreamed "stills"
you autographed were for me, glossies, glam shots, meant for me.
You signed them "Love." You signed them "Yours." In the dark
I'd lie in pain beneath powers keeping us apart for our lifetimes.
In the dark at fourteen, fifteen, and so on, dirty old men found me,
touched me, coerced me, turned off your light, and I cried.

Rob Jacques

ODE TO A BICYCLE

Hey, it's just like learning to love:
Mom and Dad clucking warnings
about hidden dangers of traffic,
learning the speeding, the falling,
the constant need to just get up,
stop crying, and get back on again.

And all of your friends tell you
their own daring, awful stories
replete with questionable advice
that doesn't apply to you anyway
about those vivid spokes, chains,
and other strange joys to avoid.

Once reckless, feckless, I fell off
and broke my damn collarbone,
but I got back on after a healing,
and still I ride over hell and back,
sometimes dangerously, foolishly
loose over gravelly, icy ground,

because I love sweating healthy,
panting, deep breathing, all of it
under stormy, rapacious skies,
the pumping going upon going,
making hot, hard, muscular work,
the hellacious burn in my thighs.

CORRALLED

Some of us like our man unmoving,
plunked down and couch-bound,
TV playing something irrelevant
and harmless like sports, our man
half-dozing, a six-pack contentment
slurred as a smile across his wet lips
as he thinks he's chosen everything,
and we feed him well, keep track
of all he thinks his needs are, see that
he's clean and comfortable and king.

Some of us like our man to nap,
and we place approving blankets
over his ruthlessly exciting body
and listen from our chair to a snore
that bespeaks flaccidity of purpose
on Sunday afternoons, fundamental
suppression of dominance and more,
and we relax in his unshaven face,
his dark nipple-circles pushing out
his tee-shirt with a feminine grace.

Some of us like our man to romp
on carefully supervised play-dates
with other closely monitored men
on Saturday's soccer fields, perhaps
on bowling-alley evenings where
energy is harmless and only pins fly,
and we hem them in as we watch,
careful to observe their exhaustion
become our elation, their tiring
our prevention of things gone awry.

Some of us know domestication
needs attention, and we study signs
long enough, well enough to see
when he's sexually restless, repressed,
about to throw off cultural strictures
with a hot illogic we can't arrest,
so we strip him and lay him, dance
making love with a loud longing,
our bodies much-willing receptacles
in which his uncivil passions prance.

YOUNG IMPRESSIONIST
For Payton

You look lovely, your wide-open eyes giving you away
as you fumble my twelve-ounce Americano decaf
(room for cream) into a paper cup, as you work
a coffee counter to pay the rent, as you fuss and muse alone
in spite of customers waiting, eyes unused to seeing ruses,
subterfuge and guile, and their innocence is romantic,
tugging idiotically at my heart, and I picture you pure
in your clinging pajamas last night, unable to sleep, thrashing
a new thought, drawing you back to that evening's canvas,
and now you stare distracted, not seeing me staring back,
as you think of artistry in your bedroom where you keep
your soul's true treasure still wet on an easel, and there
it awaits completion's soft ceremonies before you sleep.

LAZARUS

At their desks, these first-year wonders wait,
fresh from summer, still with bits of clinging Mom and Dad
not wiped clean from their new free will,
at their desks and eager, fresh, even dew-eyed,
appealing in their powerful innocence,
their bodies supple, lovely to look at and imagine feeling.

And I, their first professor, am about to speak,
to tell them everything. Unlike Prufrock, I am Prince Hamlet,
even Virgil, in my own way, leading young Dantes downward
to self-recognition, to easy virtue, to a latent dismay
with how hard sin is and how it has begun, this moralizing,
marginalized sophistry the aged give as alternative for fun.

The blond in the first row, his clear eyes big,
his lips sucking an eraser he won't need,
is ready to take notes. Ankles crossed, he leans forward
wanting to know, wanting to understand this time.
His high school platitudes behind him, he wants college truth,
his cheeks flushing with anticipation of my first word,
his back braced, his mind cleared of parental detritus,
ready now to really learn what's real and what isn't.

The brunette in the first row leans back, breasts pushing out
for no good reason, for none of the others can see her front
and they're wasted on me, as are her liquid limbs that move
smoothly through her blouse sleeves, her small feet and dainty hands
that are out of place in what I have to say, and she shakes her head
gracefully, her dark curls gently bobbing as she settles herself
to finally hear, to hear it all told boldly and well by the odd professor
who, to her, looks like a withered corpse and not at all like the blond
sitting beside her who has yet to notice all of her that I've noticed.

They look at me, the two of them, ready to welcome like the others
wisdom from wizened professors who look nothing like the living
who even now sit in the Student Union scoffing at strictures and dicta
and homework assignments that clash in the night with human arousal.
Tell them of Homer? But how? Shall I tell them how long ago
all they haven't yet imagined came to nothing?

And I have come forth out from my tomb-like room, summoned.
By whom? And to what purpose? By students, of course,
who've paid their fees and demand knowledge. By students
who think they can be taught everything. But I in my white lab coat
wound about me like a tight-fitting shroud, I with my chalk about to turn
and write my name on the board beneath course number and date,
I must disappoint, must tell them–not in so many words–
that what's worth learning cannot be taught. It sits without language
on the lips of the dead. It lies heavy in lore lost in the Big Bang.

So I have been over on the Other Side and now come back to tell you
in thoughtless language you cannot speak,
in mathematics beyond your powers of calculation,
in delicate artistry whose least tracings defy your crabbed hand,
in music you mistake for noise
and with infinite grief you can't begin to understand.

STEWART
D. ANTWAN

give me his head

D. Antwan Stewart is a native of Knoxville, Tennessee, and attended the University of Tennessee there. He graduated with an honors B.A. in English and later received fellowships from the Bucknell Seminar for Younger Poets and the Michener Center for Writers, where he earned the M.F.A. in poetry. He has authored two chapbooks, *The Terribly Beautiful* (Main Street Rag Editor's Choice Chapbook Series, 2006) and *Sotto Voce* (Main Street Rag Editor's Choice Chapbook Series, 2008). Recent poems appear in periodicals and anthologies including *Callaloo*, *Meridian*, *Many Mountains Moving*, *Poet Lore*, *storySouth*, *The Southern Poetry Anthology*, *Volume III: Contemporary Appalachia*, *The Best Gay Poetry 2008*, and *Verse Daily*.

SEX/LOVE

We're hoping to get lucky after months of foolhardy misses,
      taking our licks — that is our losses —
in stride as best we can if our best is a spectacle.
      We've never experienced the true wham-bam of love,
the turn-me-on-my-ear-&-spank-me kind of
      foolishness we drool about until our faces run like legs
in a swirled glass of wine. & who said sex & love
      were mutually inclusive? We want sex-beneath-the-bleachers-
after-the-high-school-jamboree but not the glory-hole
      vulgarity, the fingering against the stall wall.
We want a man who can't finish his after-dinner flan
      to drive us home, a man we can invite in for a glass
of Bordeaux to coax him — but not ply him —
      into a walk along the promenade, conversation
never turning to sex since in the past it's been a train wreck no one takes
      their eyes from, as though it's become the lead story
on the 6 o' clock news, with men in vestibules weeping
      because how else to bear our sex as sarcophagus
for the body — as if we were a horned-up seventeen
      wishing only for tastes of flesh? We think tonight's the night
we might get lucky. If not, we've lasted all these months now,
      never explaining our way of seeing things:
that we've always been our own best date, that
      no one woos us better than we do.

PICARESQUE

Yes, even teenaged boys kiss their pillows
as they've known their sisters to do.
I was no exception.
Only the pictures of mannequin-perfect women
on my walls that most boys would pretend
love-making—their slinky blue dresses bunched
around their waists, just barely covering their asses
like sagging skin—was more my brother's
predilection than mine—since, secretly, I
swaddled myself in the fantasy of boys
on the basketball court playing within
the chain-linked fence. Their shirts off, skins
glistened like rhinestones mined from a cave
deep within our ghetto. Their bodies swayed—
one hand gripping net-less hoops—ripened
in twilight as though any moment
they'd tattoo themselves to night's papyrus.
Surely this was girlhood whimsy: each night
sinking my head into the cold
pillow cushion dreaming of asses
barely contained in jeans they pulled up
sporadically as if to showcase the bulbous
curves with no more shame
than women on my walls cocking enough
leg to send any other boy into a frenzy.
But my glee manifested in those sweat-grimed
boys scaling fences erected
like prison bars around the neighbor-
hood while cops chased them into a choke-
hold. I'd watch just as any nosy neighbor too bored
with her own life to pay attention to it:
how they writhed beneath grips
as they'd done a thousand times before
wrestling with other boys—almost like a rite of passage in case,
one day, they'd have to fight themselves out
of juvenile hall, or worse, prison . . . which is
what I felt I was living in each time
D & I sat on the bus bench for no
particular reason other than to tell stories
of sticking two fingers in a girl's vagina

because I had to, & because D couldn't
help but be the only one of us
teenage boys to fuck a girl & have us
melting like ice cubes from the fire
of his telling, as if he were
behind the pulpit speaking the gospel
of how boys became men who fuck
as if fucking were a sacrament
meant to dissolve on the tongue.
In his gaze I became a specter
of a once-present thing. I was
no longer there—if only to fall prey
to my own self-consciousness:
remembering how I was caught once
prancing around in fluffy pink slippers,
claiming to be queen of my own parade. My father
stood there in the doorjamb with smoke
coiling around his eyes
because I was that hot,
or else he refused to believe
his own son could be a faggot.
He wanted me trapped in the shame of it
as though I were a thousand wings imprisoned
in a jar with no route to escape. So for years
I pretended to be one of D's boys,
though it couldn't last. Eventually
it became more difficult to escape men like ghosts
wandering parks in light bare enough to see
lips moving like ventriloquists beckoning me
to touch, to kneel down not in prayer
but for the promise of one's body: one man
becoming the second skin of another, to be
unafraid of cock-in-hand-becomes-mortar-&-pestle.
I could've screamed as if a mouthful of wasps
had escaped & tried to cut myself
from that scene. But using dull scissors,
I relished the difficulty in fleeing ribbons of light
unraveling shadows coming toward me
panting, eager & waiting.

A TRYST

I tried to be a gigolo once,
but neither of us knew why
I thought I'd ever be good at it:
I almost made a castrato of him
when I went down on him,
because it was my first time.
When we passed each other
beneath that barely luminous light,
I knew he'd think I'd be spectacular —
how we circled each other like secrets
circulating amongst people who refuse the truth,
needing, instead, to make up fictions.
& I've never blamed him
for sitting next to me, grimaced
& slump-shouldered in the motel,
in the well-lit savage part of the city
listening to the couple behind the paper-
thin walls fucking the way strangers do:
nothing but limbs hyphenating other limbs,
hands palming pelvises, bodies flickering
in the spotlight of cars passing by their window,
their muted screeches like traffic
of alley cats . . . I wanted to fuck him
then & there just thinking about it. & I tried,
& smiled at him, but he turned away — refusing
even a glimpse of me,
& I'd never felt so unconsidered —
as if I were a bench on which he could rest
his disregard: that this was a mistake,
that we could be nothing more than passing
acquaintances. So I waited in silence until he fell asleep —
the room being paid for through the night —
& listened to him make a noise like a walrus's
skin sliding into the muck of wet sand,
slowly circling deeper into delirium,
like his sleep, but not like sleep. Like death.
I imagined his body slowly decomposing, each chest fall
& rise another second ticked off his life.
I whispered to him, *Are you dying, leaving me,*
as if we were lovers. But he was silent despite his noise,
& I confused by how much I admired his tranquility,

how he shone in the moon's light casing
his skin, the bones of that room. I wanted to sidle up against
his body, find comfort in his stillness.
I wanted to pull him closer, to visit his body
for a while. The way long-time companions hold
each other in a swallow of light & think nothing
of the silence, how noisily its absence of sound compels one
to find comfort in the simplest gestures. But we were strangers
meeting for a quick fuck that never happened.
& I was no gigolo —
though it was a small price to pay
simply to be beside him,
covers pulled to my chin, waiting out the night.

D. Antwan Stewart

IN DEFENSE OF THE CLOSET
for Tyler Clementi

Who really needs to know the missing part of his story,
what's there locked behind the eyes, cowering —
the unsolvable riddle. Something grave peers,
blank like slate or tombstone chipped away
until only by some generous light what is spelled out
is barely understood. Why into the eyes do we
cast down our buckets? Why not into the hands
which bear the markings of minimal labor, as if
simply from a responsibility to rise from bed
each morning? Give me his head, the mop of hair
in which fingers tread strand by strand
to get to the crown at the center. Remove it
& he'll fall out of his skin, roll in the dirt,
dip in water, a new casing, entombed, embalmed
with new life. The missing part is the ragged
edges where the seams come together, smoothed.
Particles of matter, which is the soul, the better part
of the body which makes it whole, identifiable,
lie piled on the floor like rubble of ancient ruins.
Allow him this dust & you'll find a man who trusts
his own instincts enough to blink without fear
of being found out. Allow him mystery without
acknowledging the ghostlier self, to peer
as if from a window, waiting for the time when
& for whom he will open the door, cross the threshold,
or to remain locked inside, forever, for the sake of himself.

KLAWITTER
GEORGE

sweet testosterone

George Klawitter teaches literature at St. Edward's University in Austin, Texas. *Country Matters*, his first book of poetry, appeared in 2001, and his book *Let Orpheus Take Your Hand* won the Gival Press Poetry Prize in 2002. *His Noble Numbers*, his most recent book of poetry, appeared in 2011.

COUNTRY VISIT

Nude he is as delicate as a fawn
moving along the path from house to pool.
He waits for guests to satisfy his mood,
to stir the summer water, taste the wind.

Nothing for his visitors can hint
of impropriety: the wine, the food,
must be as perfect as a Persian jewel,
as flawless as an unvoiced Schubert song.

They come. They eat. They swim. They rave. They're gone.
Then he dusts the Chinese paintings where the cruel
stares of dilettantes had settled, where rosewood
begs polish where greasy fingers sinned.

By early evening sprays of mint
will balm the air no urban misfits could.
Cleanliness remains his only tool,
his only text *l'après-midi d'un faun*.

OLYMPIC HERO

You see a man, let's say
Ivan from Bulgaria, skating
Like a Cossack madman on the ice,

And your heart props to attention,
Breathing seems unnecessary,
All moments fuse to black.

He jabs a toe into the rink
And leaps spinning loops
Inside of yellow loops.

The crowd goes wild
But shutters to a purr
When your eyes close them out.

He's yours, the man in black,
The eyebrows fused, the mouth intent,
The feathers folded underneath his shirt.

JESUS' COCK

I went to an estate sale
with my friend Paul.
Inside the denuded living room
a single painting hung on the wall —
crucified Jesus totally naked,
no loincloth, no discrete shadow,
nothing but Jesus and his cock.

At last somebody got it right —
none of that stupid modesty stuff.
After all, the Bible says he was stripped.
I can't imagine the Romans
missing a chance at humiliation
of the condemned.
He was, after all,
a criminal of the vilest sort.

And anyway if his sacrifice
to the father was to be complete
He couldn't hold back anything,
not even a shred of cloth.

So there he was for three hours.
Naked.

You need more proof?
The shroud shows no sign of a loincloth.
Just the hands folded gently over the cock.

It was the only thing in the house
not for sale.
It was the only thing I wanted.

Not the dirty strings
of red and blue Christmas lights.
Not yesterday's shirts and ties.
Not the crusty pots of dead philodendron.

Just Jesus' cock.
And it wasn't for sale.

ARS GRATIA ARTIS

Each Chinese painting that he hangs
swims a delicate bird nest
into his Western soul.

The black and white of truth
untouched by color or hue
sing through line and cloud

as his love unmasked in light
opens the sun in rooms
relaxed of door and window.

To enter each scroll — an adventure.
To leave — a mystic dream.
Like his body, like his Caribbean eyes.

A MAN AT LAST

I go back in time to join the team.
The musty smell of the locker room
hits me as I slip into the dark
I never knew, the heavy stench

of adolescence pulled by window fans out
into New Orleans' unrepentant sun.
Cool in the space I can only guess
was rife with the chatty camaraderie

of boys I sat beside in Algebra and Latin
but never had the guts to talk to,
glassed as they were in their strange fervor,
patois, and uncontrollable urges,

talk of girls and week-end escapades,
bayou snakes and oyster stew,
and whores and beer and rock-n-roll
I could only scare into my mind.

Instead I lazed into the band
where chrome and clarinet were clean,
polished, meant for higher things, heaven,
above the football lair I never entered.

In the aerie I learned Sousa, Offenbach,
the thrill of conquering arpeggios Mozart
made a thousand years before, the baton
our only sign of discipline and order.

On Friday nights we'd gather in the stands
where, flashed in blue and gold and feathers,
we'd entertain the great athletic gods
who smashed themselves on the field below.

But now in dreams I'm one of them.
I don my jock and plastic codpiece,
lace my shoulder pads and place my helmet
on my Achilles' head, my feet in Hector's shoes.

We start to chant our vulgar taunts
against the enemy we plan to crush.
We're pumped on sweet testosterone,
ready for the crash of leather, cleats, and bone.

But mostly we are one, lost in one organic
will to dominate, to shine before the crowd
that cheers us into tense heroics
for the gods who'll father us into Valhalla.

TRADITION

I wonder which asshole
came up with the idea of circumcision.
Some creative idiot in ancient times
needed a ritual to weld the tribe,
so he took a stone knife to the dick.

It's not like he wanted to parade
his glans in public light
because some gourd quickly
fitted itself for the wonderment of all
who circled the bleeding patriarch.

The schmucks bought it all:
the pain, the supposed ecstasy
of ceremonial camaraderie,
the joy of communal bonding —
all a bunch of wretched hooey

so some sadist without a foreskin
but plenty of blatant power
could claim a holy vision
instructed him to cut the manhood
from every adolescent boy child.

It's a custom that should die —
along with roasted enemy flesh
and holistic shamanism
and fear and superstition —
all the trappings of the ignorant.

Instead, let's give them Mozart uncut
and Beethoven fresh from his second.
Let them glory in Picasso intact
and endless Schubert lieder.
You get the point. Let them have theirs.

THE NEWS IS EVER GOOD

Because you know my name, I'm yours, tamed
by every syllable you speak, my wildness
misted, my passion crystallized, my only
hope your passing smile, a word, my prayer

to be in covenant with you, my plan
to wait laired and panting underneath
forbidding gods and cloud-foreboding skies.

I look for signs, scan your face and eyes
to trace a signal hidden far beneath
the cream and blue of you, so man to man

we can ignite a nightly flame and dare
defy the universe of no's. Our lonely
ones becomes a one of yes, your kindness
fused into my soul, bruised and shamed.

THE SPIDER

With the most delicate of fingers
he crochets a web of words around
my aging heart. The syllables are taut,
as sparse as precious ore that ants ignore

but humans kill for. Because his memory lingers
over years, the stitching can surround
our shards of friendship, shattered here about
my mind, willing to restore

our love ruptured by the cruelty
of distance. As he spins the filigree
that sound and sense suture into lines

of verse, my eyes go dim. His royalty,
refined by years of careful ministry,
weaves the mesh embroidered with our lives.

TRIPTYCH

I. Action at the Auction

At the Art Erotica affair last night
a painting took my hand. A naked man
seated in a whirl of turquoise,
facing me with total concentration —
I have not felt so wanted in sixty years.

Of all the glamour up for sale,
hanging on the wire fences dark
against the dark dark walls
of the cavernous bunker hall
where thousands milled for charity,

of all the men who looked at me,
he alone remains deep and clear
in his intentions. It's not as if
he wants to move in with me —
he already has. I'm caught

in his acrylic gaze and realize
my life will never rest again
purposeless or mean. I'm tamed,
resolved the oil of his face will cling
inside the sour sweetness of my heart.

And so I bid the silent auction
before I slipped into the noisy quiet
of the carnival outside where revellers
moved club to club unaware
I floated through their light and joy.

Now I'll wait for days by the telephone
for a voice to say I've won the man —
he's waiting to be taken home.
My money could not buy a better lie,
those eyes alone worth the nudity.

II. The Lost Man

I rise in the middle of the night
to look for him. On every wall
the landscapes hang, the portraits,
the still lifes with their mocking
grapes and lemons, fish and tulips,

but nowhere does he wait
gently condescending
to my fervid adoration
and my daily questions, wondering
who he is or why he came to me,

nowhere does his graceful nakedness
and pony tail sanctify a corner nook,
nowhere his cock accented
with a touch of pubic black,
his arms heavy in pink and white.

When I was a little boy in the South
I'd wander every month or so
into the City Park museum where
one painting always drew me
to the angle of a quiet room:

a pleasant bishop at a table
raising a glass of wine and talking
about the ladyfingers at his reach.
That swirl of Renaissance was mine
and stays inside my brain even now.

Because I would not jack a price
at the auction, I guess I'll grow
accustomed to your absence.
You are somewhere else tonight
and just an ashen residue in me.

III. Three Days Later

My one-night stand is fading
to the honeyed regret
it will remain, a firm reminder
of my feeble needs, infantile
craving for gratification.

No amount of logic or distraction
from acquired beauties will dislodge
the lost man from the niche
where he clings cemented
on my wall of unforgiving memory,

the only remnant of our fling
in the hot and clammy chamber
of the art fair where he ruled
under his bright light as I lusted
from the floor below.

Circling like a beast obsessed,
I went and came for hours
as he watched cool,
the man in charge,
my libido perking in the April heat.

Some recollections never leave:
etched like a fine lithograph
into the fabric of my grimy brain,
they surface summoned during need
when I tremble for a touch of beauty.

To know that he exists somewhere
in his *ars gratia artis* calm
bringing someone nightly happiness
remains my only medicine for loss —
that and the recollection of our sex.

BEAM
JEFFERY

chalice of the flesh

Jeffery Beam is poetry editor of the print & online literary journal *Oyster Boy Review* and a botanical librarian in the Biology Library at UNC-Chapel Hill, North Carolina. His latest collection, *Gospel Earth*, was recently released by Skysill Press (England), as was a chaplet, *Me Moving*, from Longhouse. *An Invocation* (Country Valley Press) and *The Lord of Orchards* — a Jonathan Williams online feature (with Richard Owens) for *Jacket* magazine, were published in 2009. His other many award-winning works include *Visions of Dame Kind* (The Jargon Society), *An Elizabethan Bestiary: Retold* (Horse and Buggy), *The Fountain* (NC Wesleyan College Press), *The Beautiful Tendons: Uncollected Queer Poems 1969 – 2007* (White Crane Wisdom Series), *On Hounded Ground: Home & the Creative Life* (Bookgirl Press, Japan), *Light & Shadow: The Photographs of Claire Yaffa* (with poems by Jeffery Beam, Aperture) and an online chapbook selection from *Gospel Earth* (Longhouse). Forthcoming in late 2011 and 2012 are the following: *Midwinter Fires* (Seven Kitchens Press); *MountSeaEden* (Chester Creek Press); *The Broken Flower* (Skysill Press); a song-cycle with composer Jake Heggie, soprano Andrea Moore, and writers Allan Gurganus, Michael Malone, Frances Mayes, Lee Smith, and Daniel Wallace; and a song-cycle with composer Steven Serpa. Jeffery lives in Hillsborough, North Carolina, with his partner of 31 years, Stanley Finch.

www.unc.edu/~jeffbeam/index.html

THE LOVERS

I know not how I came of you and I know
          not where I go with
you, but I know I came well and shall go well.

- Walt Whitman

Do you remember
the afternoon
under the maples' shadows
in early autumn
in the aging arboretum,

the warm talk of brothers
just accustoming
themselves to their new
intelligence, that
unforgettable beauty?

On distant paths, separate,
they had travelled, and now,
their souls' startling interior
glimmer insinuating.
How splendidly it comes to me,

in my room, in the aging autumn,
the youthful brothers, their
darkening glances,
firm hands held
together under

common solitudes.
And the simple reverence
of blood pulsing
under the yellow maple.
The mockingbird above them.

A JAZZ FOR DOROTHY PARKER

Why should I mingle
Love with sadness

That street glance
Broke me first?

And didn't it uplift me
Make me giggle

A grown man
Nothing worse?

Why should I mingle
Love with sadness

When kisses
Rule the day?

Or celebrate the heart's
Rude madness

Because he's simply
Away?

Why should I mingle
Love with sadness

I never took the
Curse?

And, anyway,
I'm all for gladness

Even at its worst.

PRIAPEAN HYMNS

When I arise
    my buttocks mark
    my sitting place

    Taking the smooth drink
    of youth
    I become
    drunk

Bathing at midnight
    in my genital spring
    I pierce my knees with
    thorny quince

    The skin's cloth brittle

    Wind
    blow through me your
    amber teeth
    I will remove each layer
    for a balm

You do not know me
    I am your daughter

Rising quickly we
    ask
    What will our children be
    Entering the house of penitential years
    The house of beans of
    hematite
    and corn

    We beat our hands in sorrow
    long as nuthatches

    Winter
    we sit under trees
    in sleet and woe
    Spring now
    When will weeping
    end

Centuries ago
        ears of maize
        were called
        embraces
        One could wrap
        one's arms
        around them

We go to find a place to weep in our loneliness
        The garden path bordered by wild onion

I shall remain
        when the nails of the wall forget
        when the earth eats my dust
        I shall remain
        as mimosa remains
        long
        into winter

Redbud calls me son
        I answer
        He gives me this name
        for the prince who
        angers the wind with
        shameless promises
        spoken in the forsythia

I cannot tell you why but
        naked in this breeze
        my genitals roast and cure
        My body of three sexes
        writes its desire
        The honey bee
        combs my unhaired belly

Maimed and withering
        I remember
        love's inscriptions
        on your body of
        creatures
        rooted and flying
        Of ivy
        holding the stones
        together

ON A GUESS JEANS AD
for Jack Fullilove & Alain LeSage

I.

Spring in some city. Warm enough to move bed
Linens to the balcony. Warm enough, no doubt,
To lounge all day, wait for stars to come out,
Streetlights fusing in the river's evening red.

Pondering the question of his satin jeans
Some would call time well-spent, others not. Time
To enamor myself of the slim voluptuous rhyme
In his cool gaze, finger to lips, legs' sheen.

Discerning whether anticipation or loneliness
Excites him, I'm sure the pink spread
Rumpled by his dread but expectant caress

Matches the apple blossoms beyond the balcony's
Black wrought iron bars - two muscled filigrees.
Of course, his pose, all this, not to be shunned.

Not to be shunned, his pose, all this, of course,
An advertiser's ploy to arouse, charge the obvious flow,
Inner and outer. His puzzlement shows
Us contradictions we wish for; what choice

We desire. Ours, to insert into the scene.
He's beyond us, but each of us immediately remove
The jeans, yellow tank (merchandise), kiss his toes
(Shoeless to express readiness, repose). Sting

Red-blond shocks of oiled hair through our hands.
Sniff the armpit redolently shared,
Leaving only silver chain against bare tan

(hardly a line, solidly brown - if we hadn't guessed).
What price these legs, those eyes, these lips?
Could we but know his name, would he confess?

II.

It doesn't satisfy
        Oh sure
for a moment
        he's all
you see

      and then
those tight satin jeans
his naked feet
        just right for
  sucking

What a puzzled look
        half
          loneliness
half
   waiting
        seeing you from
his cramped balcony-sheeted
boudoir
     finger to lips
armpit open
      alluring

You might just
       rip them off
those jeans
      rumpling linens
while arched brows
        (blond)
  under the apple tree's pink shadow
tighten

He grips the wrought iron bars
against your weight

But wait
    it's an ad

All surface all
      Lust and Madison Avenue

It's him they want you to think
you're buying

and for a moment
                    he's all
    you see
sunning on the Seine

DICKESSENCE
for Shane Allison

I tell you the water here is the voice of becoming human
and it speaks in the name of all men!
                - René Depestre

My dick's monk-hood drops
My dick taming men startling their lunacy by the black moon on its crown
My dick's shy sleep under tawny densely-woven folds clothed
    with dull sheen
My dick a slag-coal burnt to diamond
My dick eaten by wayward denizens of dark
My dick gulped entirely in spring by the gentle shepherd
My dick's seven inches slick with heavenly angels' praise
My dick's seven inches slick with earthly angels' praise
My dick a thousand million angels shooting from its eye
My dick hooded-hard held tightly by thugs & righteous orators
My dick deep into quicksilver/cavern/honeycombs oozed with caramel
My dick worshipped by a coco gallant tattooed
    with my name & mimosa charm
My dick idolized by a pitch-black amigo tattooed
    with my name & reckless charm
My dick venerated by a coffee-colored cupid tattooed
    with my name & seductive charm
My dick revered by a sweet caffellatte amoroso tattooed
    with my name & boisterous charm
My dick sweet-talked by an espresso flirt tattooed
    with my name & luminous charm
My dick cajoled by a cappuccino darling tattooed
    with my name & holy charm
My dick caught in the groovemouth of a gorgeous Caravaggio
My dick trampolined by a blue-black caballero
    his curved cock up my sugared-ass
My dick's bass lines & drumbeats in a wrestler's turbulent throat
My dick a soft unintentional wink smearing succulent lips
My dick chorused by a tall tough's rippled waters on his satin-smooth chest
My dick novocained intoxicated erupted by a painted-rain Indian chief
My dick indigoed by a slurping riveter on high-beam steel
My dick painted with rushes made still by a merman's still-water mouth
My dick a side-winder hissing at jubilant bladed cowboys
My attracting dick wind-blown by Amerika's substantial sons
My dick burgundy for a Persian chap bound in jewels
My dick pounded asleep by my husband's throb up my tunnel

My dick slippery admiring from Shaolin dick torturing my tendered hole
My dick commended extolled honored eulogized congratulated tributed
My dick applauded acclaimed approved raptured glorified
My dick flattered buttered-up persuaded coaxed beguiled magnetized
My dick grandiosed honored exalted adored esteemed rarified
My dick Whitman's name upon it scrawled with grass blades
My dick decorated elaborated embroidered
    in the Hall of the Mountain Kings
My dick flower blooming in dark mirrors
My dick a moth fluttering between the green-grocer's & butcher's hands
My dick geranium pouring from its tip in the nursery man's palm
My dick nasturtiums decanting from its tip in the nursery man's palm
My dick grape-ivy lashing from its tip in the nursery man's palm
My dick tickled by a Nubian prince bristling my throat with his flame
My dick churned by a slight curly-haired Sicilian
    under the Chiesa's shadow
My dick's sacks carrying soft/cold/honey/heaviness mercurial globular
My dick greased with blueberries suckled by the soccer captain & his team
My dick gumming hairy thighs with hashish opium
My dick a red heart beating within him
My dick between Hades' buns drawing charcoal-down
My dick between Hades' lips drawing underworld-white
My dick between Hades' hands spewing magma onto his red-brown chest
My dick Etna glowing red with lava rain
My dick riding the stag-God's antlers
My dick caught in my hand writing a New Covenant
My dick reigning before The Great One & Lucifer for We are the Same
My dick ripple of flesh He the God

SEBASTIAN AT SIEGE

Mother, the air is a thief.
It steals salt from the body, loosens
the Will, until it splays out, liquid.
I sit straight up in bed, naked,
looking in the mirror. This, my body,
which I consume. The tendons
and frets on which it hangs.
Hating it once, it is now so beautiful, dying
in its time. Learning how to learn, to whistle
with the starlings, names a tender absolution.
In this Byzantine chamber, the air
makes a fist. An angel
bursting through the chalice of the flesh.
In these catacombs I perfect my sweat.

NO ONE ELSE WILL DO
with a nod to Gertrude Stein

I love my love with a b
because the bee stings but smells of
flowers

I love my love for trees
stand up and walk beside him
I see men as trees, walking

I love my love for a p
The prince provokes him when
the dew rises

I love my love with this and all
the other

I love him with an a
The Word created it

I love him with a zero because
I am

I love him suddenly and coarse
He should
know it

I love him with a pheasant
because Ishmael stood
the storm

Oak, cedar, birch
I love my love

Creek, rock, moss and
I do

Pear, apple, grape
He's mine

I love my love with an o
There is no other

I love my love with my cats
that I do

I do I do and here
he is a-coming

I love my love with a j
Here I join
him

I HAVE NEVER WANTED

I have never wanted to
                              write
            the perfect poem, only
the im
            perfect, as the human is
as the stone
                        underfoot's not
            perfect
                        but perfected by its being
stone:
            the poem
                              perfected
by its being
                        & me being
            human
                              also that.
I have always wanted the
                              under
            side of things, the side
shaded
            by moss, the coolness under
the walkway
                        stone, the silver &
            spotted
                        backside of the *Elaeagnus*
leaf.
            I have
                        always
wanted the elegance
                        of the unseen
            when the
                              light
first comes through & the shine
                              was
            (is) there all the time
wanted:
            I have
                        always wanted
the poem
                        perfected.

XAVIER EMANUEL

i will always be your child

Emanuel Xavier is author of the novel, *Christ Like*, the poetry collections, *Americano* and *If Jesus Were Gay & other poems*, and editor of *Me No Habla With Acento: Contemporary Latino Poetry*. Recipient of the Marsha A. Gomez Cultural Heritage Award, a New York City Council Citation, a World Pride Award, and proclaimed a GLBT Icon by the Equality Forum, he has been featured on *Russell Simmons presents Def Poetry* on HBO. His spoken word/music compilation CD, *Legendary- The Spoken Word Poetry of Emanuel Xavier*, is available for download on iTunes. He currently works for the Random House publishing company.

www.emanuelxavier.com

CONQUEST

Your absence is the pillow used to cuddle at night, with you next to
me, as the moon watches over the despair of this darkness.

Distant and cold like the snow of mountains.
It is my cue to leave in the morning.

This rose, my heart, will not have sunlight to bloom here.
Tears will not provide enough rain to sustain this life.

Your demons revel in their fire.
Your songs lure another shipwrecked soul.

Your beauty disguises your myths, like religion.
Wars waged without necessity, out of fear.

What brought us to the tomb of this bed was only meant to be a
dramatic kiss, hope between wounded soldiers on a stage.

I should have tasted the blood on your lips,
caught a glimpse of a deadbeat father in your eyes.

You shot with fair warning, celebrated your victory,
heroic in your justice of killing the child with stolen toy in hand.

I will not be meaningful enough to haunt you
beyond words and I will be forgotten.

It was not your duty to hold me in your arms
without holding back and, for this, I grant you atonement.

Like the morning sun, dreams were awakened by your light
and quickly faded as reality set back in.

There was loneliness and sadness, and you were the hope.
There was violence and pain, and you were the healing.

Others will undoubtedly drown in the sea of your emotions,
get lost in your conflicts; continue to be music for the masses.

Our time shared crossing this path was insignificant- when you get to
greener pastures, enjoy the air, breeze against your skin.

   I will perhaps be a story maybe worth sharing, nothing more.

MADRE AMERICA

If I were to give myself to you completely,
would it matter that I didn't come from your womb?
I have been thrown out of homes and abandoned by fathers
looking for a place to settle and offer what little is left of this spirit.
I speak your tongue and share the beds of your sons.
I would fight in your battles if considered man enough for you
The dead eyes of innocent faces would not haunt this empty soul
Would you be my motherland?
Would I be allowed to bathe in your oceans
without drowning in your oil spills
or washing ashore a lighter skinned slave in plastic chains?
Would you hold me when I die and grant me a final resting place?
Madre, put down that newspaper and look at me closely,
I much resemble your first kin before you were raped
I have tasted your tears and washed myself in your sorrow
Madre, would you grant me sanctuary for my sin of living?
Of loving?
Your children do not want me to be part of your history.
Your daughters do not care to heal these wounds.
Madre, remind them that I have kept you strong
I have cleansed you, fed you, kept you warm.
You made me who I am today but still, unworthy of their affection.
You were always full of love for all of us.
You raised us the same even when we took your splendor for granted.
We may not have the same blood but we are all connected.
I don't want to lose this family.
This heart belongs to you.
America, you have been my mother and my father.
The autumn leaves are falling and it is only summer.
Do not let them keep me from coming into your arms.
Do not let them imprison me with lies.
Do not let them kill me for wanting to share in your devotion.
Remind them that our differences
is what makes this home more beautiful than any other.
I am nourished and wise because of you.
I look out the window and am not afraid of the wilderness outside.
I only fear not finding my way back.
Madre, I want to stay here with the others to protect you.
I want to read your musings and hear your stories.
I want to stare out at your skies at night and lay on your lands.
Madre, I know it is not you but they that are jealous of our bond.

Madre, educate us all to understand more than one language.
I want to write poetry to someday teach in your schools.
Peace belongs to all of us because of you, madre.
America, I will always be your child.

MI CORAZÓN

I search for my soul in paintbrush strokes
listen for my muse in Mr. Softee ice cream truck jingles
smile at strangers on the subway for simple humanity
This heart seems a novelty but it continues to love

It makes children out of full-grown men
withdraws the instinctive awareness of animals
It beats enough passion to arouse poetry
etching words that mean nothing yet everything

Like drums and like songs
with the conviction of dance
Like rhythm flowing from bodies
It continues to love

It has outlived history like a vampire
blood healed and stronger with time
Beauty resounding from within
Bathed in tears and sheltered from the bruises outside

City noises drown the thumping sounds
Threatened to be frozen by bitter cold
but it beats to the tune of glimmering eyes
as it unfolds to render a lonesome petal

Concrete may not supply cushion
Perverse lights may weaken the stars it craves
Hatred may wage war and hindrance
but it continues to love
It reveals itself through a kiss
The same which often hides it
Often remembered and rather forgotten
like skyscrapers offering great views but obstructing the sky

An abandoned pier surrounded by polluted rivers
It continues to love

Walls torn down for a better view of the other side
It continues to love

Projects housing poverty and lifeless dreams

elevators hauling empty designer pockets
gateways to famine and drought
It continues to love

Into nights brightened by moon
It continues to love

Life as offered by family and friends
It is the salvation and prayer for forgiveness
It continues to love

It continues
to love

THE GIFT OF RAIN

There came a time when the risk to remain tight in the bud was more
painful than the risk it took to blossom.
                            - Anaïs Nin

The only thing queer is inhibition
Pride is the magnificent wig worn by the man who gambles living
to bring happiness to others or simply to herself
It is the freedom to explore limits and not living in fear of love

We believe like no other that we are cherished completely
No church, man, or woman could ever make us think
God or a higher being is not walking amongst us
with the colors of the rainbow

We are music, dance, poetry, art
We capture the splendor of the world around us with photography
We raise our families to believe in true equality
We pray for forgiveness, not for ourselves, but for hate
Wings are useless in darkness

In war, men are praised for killing others
In love, we are not welcome to battle
Some are more afraid of us than torture or death
Holding guns is tolerable but not holding hands
Our rights are of more concern than poverty

This journey is with each other not with children, goats, or horses
True love does not solely belong between a man and a woman
Just like great sex does not simply belong
between two men or two women
All should be admired only for humanity and condemned for lack of

This struggle is not straight girls kissing one another
for the attention of cameras or boys
It is denial or staying silent while those around you assault your soul
If it is crazy to want to share our lives with someone special,
let it be known we are all insane

If the Lord is indeed our shepherd,
let us not kill and hang him up on fences
Quoting books that suggest women always be submissive
and never wear gold or pearls
that men never shave

or wear clothes of more than one fabric seems questionable
when our youth are forced to deal with prejudice
without the support of families
that would stand by them if faced with the same discrimination
for being any other minority

Remove everything gay from culture
and there would pretty much be nothing left

Enjoy the rainfall,
for all the ruin it seems to bring,
it also supplies us with life

MISSING

I apologize to you now
for holding back what you should know
but there are too many expectations of me
that are my own fault for sharing my life in such detail.
I have never been good at keeping things to myself
publicly sharing what most would deem personal
but I'm learning to build walls again.

Those that actually read my words look between the lines,
"Is this what he is really like?" Perhaps.
One day, you will find me again at the amusement park.
I will be the little boy with the red balloon,
a runaway who found himself,
a life fulfilled prepared for death.

It was never your responsibility to save me.
Others didn't recognize me from milk cartons either.
You might think I am giving you the stink eye
when, in fact, I will no longer be just half deaf but fully blind.
I will be gone as soon as you look away.

When you spot the balloon in the sky
you will realize that it wasn't a dream.
The brightness of the sun will not wash away the red.
Someday you'll see me yet again, when the time is right.
Make sure to point me out to your friends
at the amusement park, the little half deaf blind boy
with the red balloon in front of the graffitied wall.

AMERICANO

I look at myself in the mirror
trying to figure out what makes me an American
I see Ecuador and Puerto Rico

I see brujo spirits moving across the backs of Santeros
splattered with the red blood of sacrificed chickens
on their virgin white clothes and blue beads for Yemaya
practicing religions without a roof

I see my own blood
reddening the white sheets of a stranger
proud American blue jean labels on the side of the bed

I see Don Rosario in his guayabera
sitting outside the bodega
with his Puerto Rican flag
reading time in the eyes of alley cats

I see my mother trying to be more like Marilyn Monroe
than Julia De Burgos
I see myself trying to be more like James Dean than Federico Garcia Lorca

I see Carlos Santana, Gloria Estefan,
Ricky Martin and Jennifer Lopez
More than just sporadic Latin explosions
More like fireworks on el Cuatro de Julio
as American as Bruce Springsteen, Janis Joplin,
Elvis Presley and Aretha Franklin

I see Taco Bell's and chicken fajita's at McDonald's
I see purple, blue, green, yellow and orange
I see Chita Rivera on Broadway

I am as American as lemon merengue pie
as American as Wonder Woman's panties
as American as Madonna's bra
as American as the Quinteñero's, the Abdul's, the Lee's,
the Jackson's, the Kennedy's
all immigrants to this soil since none sound American Indian to me
as American as television snow after the anthem is played
and I am not ashamed

Jose, can you see . . .
I pledge allegiance
to this country 'tis of me
land of dreams and opportunity
land of proud detergent names and commercialism
land of corporations

If I can win gold medals at the Olympics
sign my life away to die for the United States
No Small-town hick is gonna tell me I ain't an American
because I can spic in two languages
coño carajo y fuck you

This is my country too
where those who do not believe in freedom and diversity
are the ones who need to get the hell out

Emanuel Xavier

REVELATION
for Rane Arroyo

It was the chocolate brown walls he had painted
in anticipation of his lover's move from another state,
The soft cuddle of his cat laying on his chest as he read poetry
the way he had imagined his lover would
It was the way the leaves had turned
from green to yellow to red and the brutal winter
had covered the ground with a multitude of white snow
without ever hearing the sound of his voice
He reminisced about how they met and what they had promised
to each other, the trips back and forth and the plans
that had been set with bodies intertwined
looking through the branches up at the limitless sky

Now he lived alone with his pet surrounded
by the colors of this purgatory and
vases without arrangements, leaks that required fixing,
furniture lacking his scent
It had surprisingly shifted his entire balance-
another man who had simply vanished,
evaporated into the now thick air with nothing left behind
but lonely reflections in the mirror
It was death all over again, this room designed to be his coffin,
waiting for life to pass as everyone else
found love with ease and left him behind

He contemplated dating again
as soon as the bitter wind changed direction
from the city where he became a man
and each street reminded him of loss
It would be in deep brown or blue or green eyes
that he would forget the failure of fathers,
that books had been his brothers, songs had been his sisters
His touch would prove this existence
That someone was capable of loving him,
even if his background was a wild river most feared crossing

He looked to find his residence
in the words of others but found nothing
Until he came across the line, "I stop dreaming so I can return home"
Now he could believe once again without naivete
that poetry always demands all of our ghosts
Perhaps, even at this age, doubt would not delude his desire
With just one haunting sentence he was brought back to life

BORN THIS WAY

I want to breathe Rimbaud's last breath

I want to shower in Bukowski's golden piss

I want to wrap my legs around the sun and fuck it blind

I want to read Walt Whitman to the waves at Coney Island beach

I want to challenge the constraints of Catholics

I want to swim through Madonna's hair
    come out changed and reinvented

I want to run out to the rooftop and roll on broken glass
    lying there bloodied looking skyward

I want to foretell the future from clouds
    reaching out to touch God's naked body

I want to hang out with trannie hookers
    opening their homes and hearts as freely as their legs
    sleeping on floors
    surrounded by bitten off corners of condom packages

I want my Muse to make love to me
    pounding me hard with his hands at my wrist
    leaving me breathless and inspired to concentrate my faith

I want to hear him say, "I see Lorca in your eyes"

I want to love him like a little child
    troddling unafraid thru the heaven of his soul
    with whispers gone before nightfall

I want to hitchhike through the heart of America
    but the cars keep passing by

KAMINSKI
JAMES

orange and red portrait

James Kaminski, whose work is featured on the cover of this issue of *Assaracus*, offers us his biography in the form of a poem by his friend, Rick Branch.

http://kaminskidesigns.com

ON JIM KAMINSKI
A Poem by Rick Branch

Tweed Jackets from Army Surplus
Cloak of creativity
Oil elbow patches rest on table
Arm terminates with scotch and rope.
Muscling creation into submission
It drive it and it drives.
Hours pass — Eyes heavy — Sight without end.
Inhale thru rope hole
Kiss canvas with dry mouth
Shake off crumbs and crouton bits
Creatures emerge from oil broth, humming crows.
Light screams spirits.
Angles weep dark snarls
Nothing forgives unbound.
Seep with the marmalade foam.
Wake like animal in heat — repeat.
Paint again with brain torn sinew.

SUBMIT TO ASSARACUS

The mission of Sibling Rivalry Press is to develop, publish, and promote outlaw artistic talent — those projects which inspire people to read, challenge, and ponder the complexities of life in dark rooms, under blankets by cell-phone illumination, in the backseats of cars, and on spring-day park benches next to people reading Wilde and Crane. We encourage submissions to *Assaracus* by gay male poets of any age, regardless of background, education, or level of publication experience. Submissions are accepted during the months of January, May, and September. For more information, visit us online.

SUBSCRIBE TO ASSARACUS

You asked. We delivered. We've made our mark and are ready to announce that readers can now subscribe to receive a year of *Assaracus*. The subscription price is $50.00 for US readers and $80.00 for international readers (including shipping), which buys you four book-length (120+ pages), perfect-bound issues of our grand stage for gay contemporary poetry. Subscriptions are available through our website.

www.siblingrivalrypress.com

WHAT IF YOUR HEAVEN IS YOUR HELL?

In Nashville

At the Silver Saloon, you show me
what a white boy in Wrangler Jeans
can do with my moves. The electric
slide grinds with boot scootin' boogie.
Two steps to the left, a sunburned woman
outdoes me entirely, throws in some hip
just to call me out. And I feel a bit
betrayed, dancing in this crowd
of snake-skin boots and red, white, and blue
rebel tattoos with the moves I thought
I had some kind of claim to, a way
                of mapping out hell with my feet.

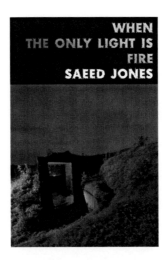

When the Only Light Is Fire by Saeed Jones
ISBN: 978-1-937420-03-1
Cover Photograph by Christopher Benbow
$12.00; 44 Pages
Available November 2011 from Sibling Rivalry Press

Lightning Source UK Ltd.
Milton Keynes UK
UKOW041815040113

204429UK00001B/179/P